Broken Bricks Still Build

REBUILDING YOUR LIFE FROM THE SHATTERED PIECES

SHAWNA-KAY SCARLETT

Broken Bricks Still Build

Trilogy Christian Publishers

A Wholly Owned Subsidiary of Trinity Broadcasting Network

2442 Michelle Drive, Tustin, CA 92780

For information, address Trilogy Christian Publishing

Rights Department, 2442 Michelle Drive, Tustin, CA 92780.

Trilogy Christian Publishing/ TBN and colophon are trademarks of Trinity Broadcasting Network.

For information about special discounts for bulk purchases, please contact Trilogy Christian Publishing.

Trilogy Disclaimer: The views and content expressed in this book are those of the author and may not necessarily reflect the views and doctrine of Trilogy Christian Publishing or the Trinity Broadcasting Network.

10 9 8 7 6 5 4 3 2 1

Library of Congress Cataloging-in-Publication Data is available.

ISBN 979-8-89333-705-1

ISBN (ebook) 979-8-89333-706-8

Dedication

I dedicate this book to those who have been broken and grapple with hopelessness and disappointments. To those who have endured the adverse effects of broken homes. To those who are fatigued by depression and rejection. To those who have lost their confidence and identity. To those holding back the silent tears from trauma. To those who are single and waiting for a spouse and a family. To the women who battle with the shame, embarrassment, and low self-esteem associated with domestic violence and sexual exploitation. To those seeking to elevate their faith or straddling the fence about their faith in Jesus Christ.

Here is my story, an open book to offer a point of reference for your circumstances.

Acknowledgments

I want to express gratitude to God for His faithfulness through the hills and valleys of life. It is because of His grace and unconditional love that this book has come to fruition. I thank God for ordering my steps as I navigated various seasons of life. Throughout my journey I had the privilege to carry everything to God in prayer because I trusted in Him. I thank God for His better plan that proves destinies do exist. Moreover, I thank God for elevating my faith and for access to the wisdom, solace, and reassurance that is available in Him.

My first lessons and values were instilled by my parents. I would like to thank my parents, Conrad Scarlett and Rev. Dorothea Walcott, for the support, life, and Godly principles they taught me throughout the years. What would life be without siblings? I would like to extend thanks to my siblings Conrad Scarlett Jr., Dr. Shanice Scarlett, Sasha-Kay, and Su-Jazz Scarlett for being lifelong friends who helped to build social skills and provided an outlet for laughing out loud. Thank you to my stepmother Misha Scarlett, who always availed herself to assist me with my academics throughout my primary and high school years.

Thank you to my mentor Pastor Teriece Murray and the elders of the faith who continue to nurture the masses. I appreciate and admire the longevity of your faith that has strengthened me and provided many points of reference on my journey.

Thank you to my fellow Jamaicans for your online presence that kept me tethered to home while being away in a foreign land. Though so far away, your presence provided a warm embrace from a distance.

To my professional colleagues, I thank you for your expertise in pedagogy. Being an educator is no easy feat. Throughout the years, I have been able to sharpen my pedagogical acumen by gleaning from your knowledge and years of experience. Thanks to my students who taught me that there is always something new to learn and increased my awareness on cultural diversity. Gracias!

Thank you to my publisher for making this project become a tangible product in the hands of readers. Finally, thanks to my readers. Some stories are reserved for the reader, the reader who reads to the end. Thank you for reading to the end. I hope my story has empowered you to rebuild your life from the shattered pieces!

Preface

In *Broken Bricks Still Build* Shawna-Kay Scarlett shares her testimony of how Christ restored her hope and confidence in Him. Christ healed her heart and empowered her to tell her story. This book will help readers recognize that:

» our stories don't end in the broken seasons, instead our stories continue to unfold

» restoration is available in Christ for us to rebuild our lives from the ashes of the past

» valley seasons will grow pale and will be remembered as waters that have passed away

Broken Bricks Still Build is a testament that God is with us through the ebbs and flows of life. With this consciousness, we can honor and worship God as the God of the hills and valleys.

Introduction

The aim of this book is to inspire God's way from the perspective of someone who lived a broken life of low self-esteem, hopelessness, and despair for many years. This book is geared towards providing encouragement and empowerment, especially for those who have experienced seasons of turbulence and turmoil. I hope that people from all strata of life will be inspired by my story of rebuilding my life from the shattered pieces. My journey showcases how I maneuvered the vicissitudes of life that tried to thwart me from experiencing God's best for me. Overcoming the valley experiences of childhood trauma, a harrowing romance, depression, and injustice was only possible through God's intervention in my life. The trajectory of my life shifted when God intercepted this path of depression, regret, low self-esteem, and low self-worth. I started to see the break of day when my eyes were propped open by gentle nudges from Christ, who began to lift my head. This impromptu encounter with Christ showed me that all along God had a greater plan than the plans I had for my life. The way my story unfolded proved that His thoughts and His ways are not mine; instead, they far exceeded all I could ever imagine for my life. I share my story to expose the truth that beauty for ashes does exist. Moreover, it is anticipated that the contents of this book will help to galvanize, grow, support, and nurture the faith of believers, unbelievers, and those straddling the fence in their faith of Jesus Christ. My greatest desire is to fulfill the mandate of spreading the gospel through this window of my life by inspiring readers to become tethered to God through Jesus Christ. I believe it is part of my mission to instill hope in the hopeless through my story. I see it necessary to motivate those who have experienced valley seasons of brokenness through my story. My testimony shows that in life, though we sojourn through the valley seasons, brighter days are coming. Regardless of the experiences that break us, no one should think that their story is over. In Christ there is restoration available that will empower us to rebuild our lives from the shattered pieces. Once we have life, God-the Potter- is still shaping our stories. God works patiently to restore us because He knows we all have need for a measure of grace. As we walk with Christ, stitch by stitch He mends the wounds of the past, for He is close to the brokenhearted. In Christ we have the privilege to live again and rise from the ashes of past pain. It is amazing how Christ transformed my scars into a story to uplift those bounded, intimidated, and embarrassed by the valley experiences of life. This book is not just a story, it is evidence of the goodness of God.

CONTENTS

Chapter 1

―∞―

Upper Parade Street

I am so glad that our Father in heaven
Tells of His love in the Book He has given;
Wonderful things in the Bible I see,
This is the dearest, that Jesus loves me.

Phillip P. Bliss

Childhood is often filled with innocent, carefree living. I was not overly concerned about the future or the issues of life. As a child, I could not perceive the significance of my experiences. The pains of my childhood were brushed off and left unprocessed. Inevitably, these childhood pains were buried in my heart while life progressed. The cavities of past trauma gradually eroded my confidence, self-esteem, and world view. As a child, I did not imagine the negative impacts of future pains. Eventually, the trauma of my childhood collided with the trauma of my adulthood and wrote a story of rebuilding life from the shattered pieces. My story became like a fire shut up in my bones (Jeremiah 20:9 NIV). I had to refrain from holding it in by finally allowing my life to become a story that tells of God's goodness. In essence, even though we are broken, we can rebuild ourselves through Christ. As a young girl from Jamaica, I had no inkling that my life would be assembled as a story to tell. The unsuspecting mundane and insignificant moments turned out to be pivotal points in the journey. The moments of confusion, pain, and waywardness were intercepted by Christ, which led to being redeemed with a purpose. I did not recognize I had a story to tell until Christ started to mend the shattered pieces of my heart and lifted my head from the valley of depression and hopelessness. In this book, I will take you on a journey of how I was able to rebuild my life from the broken pieces of a hurting heart.

"I can do all things through Christ who strengthens me."

Philippians 4:13 (NKJV)

The memories of my childhood are filled with going to church, school, and playing with my siblings. My formative years were spent in Trelawny, Jamaica, living with both parents as well as my two siblings. Being the second of three children, I shared childhood memories with my older brother and younger sister. Growing up, I remember my father as a hardworking and very disciplined man and mother as a Christian woman of God who was always praying and fasting. My father was the breadwinner of our household who made his income by being a musician, while my mother was our homemaker and nurturer. Being a skillful pianist, my father saw it necessary to teach my siblings and me the art of playing the piano. Playing the piano is one of my favorite things to do. I was always trying to learn fancy songs I would hear through media platforms or searching through the many piano books my father had in his collection.

Our backyard held so many memories. It was in the backyard that we had our German shepherds that were caged in their kennel or where we would play for hours with our neighbors. I can also remember my mother washing my hair and my sister's hair in our backyard on Saturdays which would be combed on Sunday evenings after church. Again, in our backyard we had swings, played cricket, played school and church of course. Almost every day we played school, with my sister being one of the two human students and my neighbor the other. The chairs, trees, doors and even the walls would be students that surely received floggings every time. How could I forget the mango trees in our backyard, which we enjoyed during the summer when it was harvest time.

It was customary for my siblings and me to get our clothes and shoes ready for church on Saturday evenings, because going to church on Sunday morning was non-negotiable. It was a fixed part of our lifestyle. However, it did not feel forced, neither did it feel like a chore since it was intertwined in our way of life. On Sunday mornings my siblings and I would head off to Sunday School and my mother would come later after us. In general, we would walk to church carrying our Bibles and a little purse with our offerings. We would walk to church both Sunday morning and Sunday night. During our night walks to church, we would watch and measure our shadows in the moonlight with frolic; I guess this was something to look forward to.

Church was a big part of our lives, and my favorite part was offering time. Why? We got the chance to walk up to the altar to give our offering and to listen as the choir ministered in song. I also enjoyed watching the choir as they marched in at the beginning of the service. Each member was dressed in their robes, with everyone marching in the same rhythm as the musicians played with such liveliness. How can I forget the singing of the hymns? Oh, how I loved this part of the service. We sang from the Pentecostal hymnal with such joy and vibrance, shaking of the tambourines and clapping our hands. Now, when it was time for preaching it seemed as though the service had no end. Eventually my sister and I became a part of the children's choir and participated in our annual Christmas program at our church. Then, we had baptism. One Sunday, the majority of the children and young adults were scheduled for water baptism, my sister and me included. Interestingly, everyone got baptized except for me. I stepped into the pool and started to cry. I told the minister that I changed my mind. At that time, I was about eight years old.

After returning home from church, my siblings and I would prepare for school the next day and church again in the evening. It was routine for us to have dinner at our dining table together as a family. Our dining table would also be switched to a study area, where my siblings and I would complete our homework. My father was a disciplinarian, so our homework had to be completed and being respectful was mandatory. There was a firm emphasis on education in our household. My father was intentional about preserving our textbooks to secure them for the younger children. It had always been my father's mission to ensure that we had all supplies, uniforms, books, and shoes needed for school. My brother and I attended the same all-age school, and we walked daily to school. We had to cross busy main roads, so my brother always took a firm grip on my wrist.

I always put up a resistance because I wanted my own autonomy. My brother knew better and never released my hand until we were safely on the other side of the road.

Monday nights were my father's night off from work. During these nights we would have family time where Daddy would tell us stories. We all gathered and listened attentively, because we all anticipated laughing out loud in the end. Additionally, we would have sing-a-longs as Daddy played the piano with such exuberance. We clung to the pages of the song books with efforts to keep up with the lyrics of the songs. Daddy was a jovial person and was an expert in getting a smile to wrinkle up our faces. How can I forget the donkey rides on Daddy's back, the lessons of riding a bicycle or swimming? The countless treats like ice cream left in the freezer while we slept in the night, playing board games, and our many trips to the beach. Occasionally, on Monday nights Daddy would take us to Montego Bay in the city, driving his Hillman Hunter. My sister and I would have slept through the journey because it was a long drive.

My mother was always a praying woman. I can recall countless occasions where my mother would pray over us and anoint us with olive oil, while speaking in tongues. Prayer meetings were frequent in our house. We had to read Bible verses even though we did not understand the text, and go down on our knees to pray in our living room. At times we even held hands forming a circle to pray and sing worship songs. I can remember vividly we were once studying the Book of Acts. I had no idea what Acts was about, but Mommy kept guiding us through this entire book chapter after chapter. There was a time when my mother decided that everyone in our household would be on a fast until midday. I wondered to myself how this was possible. I wondered, will we survive? Indubitably, we all went on the fast and lasted until midday. Naturally, my siblings and I waited with immense anticipation for the soup and bread to break that fast. I will never forget that experience of my first fast; it certainly was not my last. My mother always filled our house with gospel music like the albums of Kirk Franklin that we listened to on CDs and various sermons on TBN. As a little girl, it was on TBN that I first knew about Bishop TD Jakes. Seeds were being planted in my siblings and me from every direction, even from the movies we would watch on VHS tapes such as *Samson and Delia, Noah's Ark, Moses,* and *Joseph.*

Things turned for the worse when our family started to experience challenging times and suffered from the darts life targeted at us. Our family eventually succumbed to the pressures where my parents separated and later got a divorce. My mother, sister, and I moved out from our home and started an unknown journey ahead of us. At this time, I was only in the 6th grade when I had to take on new roles helping my mother and sister. My mother was now a single mom with two girls. My sister and I always prioritized getting our homework done and studying for upcoming tests. These years were filled with undeniable challenges and struggles. We experienced financially austere circumstances where our bills were not always paid on time, neither did we have the luxury of having the finest things. Nevertheless, my sister and I kept focused on our education, which paid off as we both benefited from scholarships for our tertiary education; that cushioned the expenses for our parents. Despite the challenges, my sister and I had to ring in each New Year in fine style. Clinging together, our champagne glasses filled with soda, became our tradition while watching fireworks on TV.

It is in retrospect that I truly recognized and appreciate the values my parents instilled in me regardless of the friction in our family. Most of these values never unraveled until my late twenties. Many seeds were planted in my heart that have stayed with me until today. I was oblivious to some of the seeds my parents planted, as they never germinated until the conditions were ideal. I am forever grateful that I was able to glean a plethora of wisdom from their advice, experiences, and navigation of life. Dear parents, plant seeds in your children while they are young and innocent, seeds that they may not see, recognize or understand; for in due season those embedded seeds will germinate and take root within them. When the circumstances are optimal, not necessarily amicable, these seeds will be activated. Once these seeds are quickened, fruits will spring forth that will guide, build, inspire, and give them wisdom. Parents, hide these little seeds in your children. Some seeds will be what you say, some will be your daily routines, some will be your perseverance and dedication in unprecedented times of struggles. Parents, you may not have riches in currency as your legacy for your children, but you can certainly leave a rich legacy of seeds you hide and bury deep inside them. Eventually, when the ultimate circumstance arrives, those hidden seeds will be awakened.

"Children, obey your parents in the Lord, for this is right. 'Honor your father and mother' -which is the first commandment with a promise- 'so that it may go well with you and that you may enjoy long life on the earth.'"

Ephesians 6:1-3 (NIV)

Chapter 2

———∞———

Children in the Shadows

His ear is always open, my soul need not despair,
Because my Lord and Savior, can hear a whispered prayer.

-Johnson Oatman

As my parents navigated the challenges in their marriage, they inadvertently caused distress to the front row onlookers. At the height of their raging emotions, my siblings and I became the children in the shadows. As my parents transitioned to being separated, it was a very uneasy and unsettling time. I was unhappy and felt sick a lot. I remember telling my mother that it felt like a huge lump was stuck in my chest. I never understood what was happening to me, but I knew it was associated with the unrest in our family. With the divorce of my parents, my family was now irreparably broken. I had to tag along with a laceration down the center of my body. It felt like I was playing the role of being invincible because I had to move on in life with raw wounds. With our family being disassembled, it was inevitable that I would have to take on new roles in our restructured household, which now had my mother, sister, and myself. Being the elder sister, I was responsible for overseeing the house until my mother got home from work. More responsibilities were being delegated to me until I became accustomed to running several errands for our household. I learnt to take charge from an early age, which was transferred into different aspects of my life as I transitioned from teenage years into adulthood. The subsequent years after my parents' divorce were tough, especially because we moved a lot from one house to another. I felt unstable each time we had to pack our things and head towards our next stop. During this time, I felt unsettled, anxious, and sad. I always wondered where I would call home after returning from college. The remainder of our childhood was spent between both parents, but where do I really call home? One moment we were spending time with my father and then the next we were moving to a new house. I despised the moments when I felt dragged between both parents, not knowing whose side to choose. It was not easy; at times I would just break down in tears. The despondency led to hurt and had driven an invisible wedge between me and my parents. As a child, what could I do, since there were few opportunities to express these feelings? My only option and choice was to bury the hurt deep down without uttering a word, as I moved along obliging to their directives. I never had a voice to make known the issues of my heart, so I just carried them for years buried on the inside. The reality is many of the conflicts cannot be unseen, most of which are still clear images in my mind even decades later.

The unspoken hurt and unaddressed trauma caused resentment and rebellion in me towards my parents and so the relationship between my parents and me had changed forever. When we moved out, I was never the same. My teen years were the toughest, but as I got older and matured, I learnt to suppress my emotions of anger, masked as being stoic and reserved. I mustered up the courage to get through special occasions like Christmas, birthdays, Mother's Day, and Father's Day. At the same time, I remembered my mother calling my father on several occasions to come and get me because we would have frequent arguments. So, I would pack my things and my father would come to pick me up. I would stay with him for a while and then a few weeks later I would be back with my mom. It would not be long after that my mother and I would have another episode. Throughout the years, it seemed like everyone was ignoring the elephant in the room, where the conversation was never held around the separation of our family and the subsequent divorce. I guess we were the children and so an explanation to us was not warranted.

With the separation of our family, my father's attention was diverted to his new family. I felt so unprotected since my father was no longer in our household. Normally, my father would ensure that our doors were closed every single night and that we were safe. Formerly, I felt secure knowing that Daddy would check on us at night before he went to bed after a late night at work. But now that was no longer the case. Our home was disassembled, and Daddy was no longer there. I felt unprotected and uncovered. Therefore, I assumed the responsibility to check our doors and windows at night in order to feel a sense of security. I hoped that this would allay some of my fear and anxiety. Sigmund Freud, an Austrian neurologist, once said: "I cannot think of any need in childhood as strong as the need for a father's protection." This statement resonated so deeply with me because it became true in the moments when I needed it, but it was not there. I was protecting my sister at school, on the road, and at home until my mother came from work. But who was now protecting me? To add insult to injury, my mother's brother started to live in our home for a period of time. I never saw the need to view his presence as dangerous. After all, he was my uncle—a male figure in the house who in my eyes could potentially offer some support. Alarmingly, my uncle made a sexual advance at me. This experience amplified the feeling of being unprotected and preyed upon. My uncle's sexual advance was extremely unexpected, shocking, and disturbing. I was so confused and nervous. His approach was laced with stealth as he seductively looked at me lying on the couch. He said to me that he had something to say to me, but I should not tell anybody. He emphasized that I must swear to God that I would tell anyone, not even my mother! He added that it must be a promise, so I said, "OK, I promise." He was so nervous.

So, I said, "Who or what are you talking about?" I asked him about several things, and he said it wasn't about any of those things. So, I said, "What is it?"

He said, "It's about me." Right there and then my heart was beating so hard and fast. He said it's something he would like to do. Then he said, "Never mind, next time I'll tell you" and then he walked away. I instantly sat up straight on the couch because I immediately sensed his intentions. A cloud of great panic came over me and I recognized I was in a crisis. It was a moment of fight or flight. I chose flight, and rushed outside in my uniform without any shoes as I started to cry. I headed on the road and without hesitation called my mother. I told her that I needed to talk to her about her brother and she immediately knew what was going on. So, I lingered on the road, walking around window shopping in different stores to pass time until she came in from work.

When my mother came home and confronted him, he totally denied everything, saying that wasn't what he meant. My mother was relentless. She kicked my uncle out of the house and told him he could not sleep there, not even for the night. He was in and out packing his things. I didn't go to sleep until he was done, and my mother locked him out. For days I was traumatized and found comfort in sharing with my friend who had just migrated to America. I sent her a long email telling her all the details of the ordeal I had experienced.

With my mother striving to establish independence and stability, she embarked on an educational journey to further qualify and elevate herself. This meant that my sister and I stayed at my father's house in the evenings until she got home from night class. This required new adjustments again for us and added to the instability as we navigated life between both of our parents. When my parents got divorced my brother stayed with my father, while my mother, sister, and I lived separately. With this division of our family my brother would visit us every night, if possible, by walking or riding his bicycle. Then whenever it was hurricane season my brother would batten down our windows and keep us company until the storm had passed. There would be several blown-down trees due to the hurricane that my brother would use a machete to chop into smaller pieces, so he could clear the yard of the debris. In addition, our fencing would also be torn down by the heavy winds and strewn across the yard. My brother would do his best to reassemble it in efforts of making us feel safe and secure. As I watched my brother do his best for us in these predicaments, I can now see that he was substituting for the role of my father. My brother recognized the dilemma and stepped up to fill the void in our household.

My sister and I had many other disappointments, such as the several occasions where our utilities were disconnected. Our attendance at church also dwindled drastically. I can recall my father would persistently ask us if we were attending church. Our answer would be no. We did not attend Sunday School or children's church and neither did we participate in the children's choir. It was a hot mess. Consequently, my father started to invite us to the local Methodist church on Sundays, for which he was the organist. Initially, I would always complain to my father that the Methodist church was too boring, and I could not manage to sing the high notes of the hymns. Gradually, our experience in attending the Methodist church became serendipitous. The collision into those old Methodists hymns galvanized my interest in singing those high notes, as well as developing a genuine love and appreciation for hymns. I can never forget cheerfully singing an all-time favorite, "*I am so Glad that Jesus Loves Even Me.*" As time progressed, I was uncertain if I enjoyed singing the hymns more or watching my father with adulation as he enthusiastically played the organ. I did not know that such deep hurt and love could coexist in the same heart. Deep down I always loved my father, but simultaneously there was a fathomless hurt that originated from the crumbling of our family.

Children in the shadows are often tainted by the decisions of their parents. There was a time after my parents' divorce that we had fallen into really hard times. During this time, my sister and I were now living with my father and his wife. I did not like this arrangement at all. The household did not feel like a family unit. I was a brokenhearted young girl grappling with the fragments of my family, and I became a rebellious teenager. This resulted in discord in my father's household and climaxed to the point where my father sent me back to live with my mother. My bitterness grew deeper, and it felt like a spear was used to pierce my soul. This created another layer of separation between my father and me. I packed my bags with immense disappointment in my heart and disbelief that my father was really sending me away. My sister and I were now separated for the very first time. She was left with my father, and I was now being dropped off at another parish with my mother.

I have dedicated this chapter to illuminate some of the effects that broken families have on children that are often not considered. As a child there are many things that I saw and experienced that are unforgettable and had very lasting impressions on my life. The conflicts and decisions of my parents were not always conducive to the nurturing of my siblings and me. We had to overcome the side effects of unsuitable decisions and conflicts as we stood in the shadows. I consider it a privilege to share this perspective on behalf of all children who have endured similar circumstances. This chapter also serves to encourage parents, or expectant parents, to exercise some caveat as they navigate their relational journey that involves children. This chapter would not have been possible without the events that took place in my family. So, I give credit to these memories that can be used today to provide insight and give a voice and recognition to all the children in the shadows.

This chapter also captures how some of the events of my childhood have shaped me in becoming the person I am today. The experience of being a child in the shadows informs many of my life's decisions and has provided me with a vantage point in dealing with children and young adults who are from broken families. I am more patient and understanding because I can relate from first-hand experience to the impacts of broken families. Moreover, this empathy has been extended to single mothers who are struggling to make ends meet. Divorces can be cataclysmic, and as a child in the shadows, I have the quintessential voice to unpack some challenges of broken homes.

Chapter 3

———∞———

Work in Progress

My hope is built on nothing less
than Jesus' blood and righteousness;
I dare not trust the sweetest frame,
but wholly lean on Jesus' name.

-Edward Mote

Throughout the span of my childhood and teenage years, it was always reiterated to me that I should be organized and have excellence in whatever I did. Both my parents emphasized the importance of showing up well and being polished in character. Ever since I was a little girl, my parents impressed upon my siblings and me the necessity to adequately prepare for school the night before. These practices are the fundamentals that still guide me today in being prepared for the day ahead. I have always been keen on personal presentation and how I interact with people, whether socially or professionally. I have grown to realize that personal and professional development is ongoing and is of the utmost importance. Personal refinement influences how I show up to the world and the impact I have on those I interact with. While growing up in Jamaica, I always heard the famous saying *"good manners will carry you through the world."* I have always aspired to be of good character and was intentional in adapting to new habits I deemed modest and elegant.

As a young girl, I had so much self-doubt that led to low self-esteem. I can clearly remember an awakening I got while in high school. I came across *America's Next Top Model,* where Tyra Banks was the host. There was something about her that kept me glued to this TV show and listening to her. It was the way she spoke to the young ladies; she spoke to the real person on the inside of them amidst all the shyness, timidity, and self-doubt. It was as though she was standing in my living room giving me the motivational speech to jumpstart my journey of self-confidence and self-discovery. After listening to Tyra, I felt like I could do anything. I would look in the mirror and face my insecurities with improved perspectives and acceptance. Later, I found the *Tyra Banks Show* on cable TV. I would tune in on time to ensure that I was able to view the entire show. Encountering Tyra Banks was a pivotal moment in my life that changed me forever. As a timid young girl with so many insecurities, my self-esteem and worth were gradually sculpted as I was mentored by Tyra through her shows. Looking back, I recognize that Tyra was a voice I needed to hear to help build my self-confidence. My confidence grew and developed as I left high school and started college.

Dedication was always one of my strong points, underscored by the belief that everything I do must be done in its entirety and in excellence. Being thorough has reaped so many benefits, as leaving no stone unturned is always the goal. This attribute of dedication and commitment has rewarded me with being detail oriented, organized, and objective, all of which have overflowed to my personal, social, and professional life. I have always strived to have healthy professional relationships with colleagues and just about anyone I meet. Refinement is a process which can only be cherished in hindsight after developing integrity, reliability, and impeccable work ethic. I have grown to be intentional in my efforts and to continuously strive for excellence.

"Whatever your hand finds to do, do it with all your might, for in the realm of the dead, where you are going, there is neither working nor planning nor knowledge nor wisdom."

Ecclesiastes 9: 10 (NIV)

I was always the person who sought more, more in knowledge and just to be sharpened in any way possible. It was as though I had a built-in desire for upliftment and improvement. I know I was looking for something but was not quite sure of what that was. I started off by reading self-help books, which would birth new inspiration at the end of each chapter. The more books I read, the more I wanted to hear the advice of those who have gone ahead of me; therefore, I had a heightened desire to read books. I kept the search going and then I stumbled across content creators on YouTube who proclaimed positivity, personal development, motivation, and personal faith journeys. I was enthused, and so I kept listening. I eventually joined online communities and attended conferences with like-minded individuals that further aided my personal refinement.

A great deal of my personal development is attributed to being a part of online communities. Furthermore, I was impacted by online interviews with pastors and other mentors. Being able to hear their testimonies gave me the guidance I needed to follow through and hold on to my promise by faith. In times of questions, doubts, discouragement, and pondering if my promise was worth holding on to, there was always a word that reassured me. In the background, my faith and hope were being refined each time as I received encouragement from scripture. As I listened to the interviews of pastors, I gleaned gems that will forever be rooted in my character and the process of my journey to my purpose. My faith and hope were also refined as I listened to sermons and podcasts where I was mentored from a distance. I would even join in fasting with online communities as well as take part in holy communion. There were times I had full-service encounters in my living room, bathroom, bedroom, and even in my car.

My confidence elevated throughout the years as I read more books, attended conferences, and grew to discover and love self. One of the major reasons I became a confident person was because I learned to block out the noise of negativity from naysayers. I had to allow positivity to be the dominant voice that dictates my choices and actions. *The Confident Woman Devotional,* written by Joyce Meyer, concretized and reinforced this journey of self-confidence. It was a long read, in fact a journey through 365 devotionals. Each devotional served the purpose of cementing confidence each day through God's Word.

As I evolved and gained self-confidence, I realized I had value to add to the lives of others. A part of being polished and refined was to be an asset to my career, family, personal relationships and to society at large. I pursue excellence in all things and strive to maintain a character of decency and integrity. One of the greatest contributions to the development of my character was that I recognized the need to be a good steward over the sacrifices made and lessons taught by my parents. It would be remiss of me to overlook and disregard their contributions that served as threads woven into the fabric of my character. Because of this I honor my parents. Did we go through challenging moments? Absolutely! Nevertheless, I will forever respect and honor them because all along I was standing on their shoulders, and I still do today.

The transition from dull to polished was a metamorphosis that progressed over time with maturity, personal experiences, and self-discovery. Most of my evolution did not happen in the crowd but in isolated places. In this transformation, I was delicate and vulnerable, because I had so many rough edges that needed to be refined and polished. Many times, I would withdraw from certain settings because I was not confident due to my shortcomings. I have come a long way, but there is still more work to be done. I'm still being refined, still being polished. I am proud of the lady I have transformed into today. The young, insecure girl in me never imagined that she would blossom into the confident woman I am today. Little did she know that diamonds start out rough and unrefined, but their sparkle depends on their flaws. Sometimes when I reflect on the woman I have become, I am in disbelief. The young girl who hopelessly struggled with self-confidence, self-love and worth—she's unrecognizable!

"The sparkle depends on the flaws of a diamond. Don't deny your flaws."

-Tazarra Berrien

Chapter 4

---⋈---

Hope Deferred

Be still and know that I am God.
Be still and know that I am God.
Be still and know that I am God.

-Psalm 46:10 (KJV)

During my early years of high school, I wanted to become a pianist. As I got more exposure to different disciplines, my career interest evolved to where I gravitated towards the sciences. I became enthusiastic about science class, particularly biology, and developed a passionate desire to become a dentist. When we had career week at our school, different universities did presentations and conducted symposiums to showcase various program offers. The representatives also provided pamphlets with information on the requirements for varying career choices. With curiosity and excitement, my friends and I perused the brochures to find out the prerequisites for our individual career interests. Consequently, I completed biology, chemistry, and physics in the Caribbean regional exams during my senior year of high school.

At the end of my high school career, I received competency in all examinations. I took these specialized classes with the expectation of matriculating into dentistry. In addition, I completed and submitted an application for the dentistry program at one of the universities from the symposium. Later, I received an acceptance letter into the dentistry program. I cannot say I received what was supposed to be good news in high spirits. By this time, my dream and hope of becoming a dentist was intercepted by daunting financial constraints. As a result, I opted to work for one year after leaving high school. I hoped that the finances of my parents in the next year would have afforded me the opportunity to pursue dentistry. I applied for several jobs and got no feedback. I felt less than when I saw all my other classmates pursuing higher education in tertiary institutions. I thought everyone else was on the road of achieving their career goals except for me. I felt left out and left behind. It was as though my dreams were completely shattered. This sheer disappointment felt like a wrong turn. This unexpected turn was camouflaged as a detour to purpose.

Eventually, I enrolled in the National Youth Service Program. The aim of this initiative by the Jamaican government was to prepare youths to make a valuable contribution to their community and the nation at large. Upon successful completion of this program, youths like me were equipped with life coping skills that cultivated personal and career development. During the enrollment process there were two programs available. One was the option to be an assistant in a science-related field and the other was to be a teacher's assistant. Of course I went after the science related field; however, this program was no longer being offered until the next cycle. I decided that I would not delay in waiting for the next cycle, therefore by default I signed up for being trained as a teacher's assistant. The program got started and training was underway. Upon completion of the training sessions, I was assigned to a primary school where I worked collaboratively with a certified classroom teacher.

As a trainee, I had the chance to understudy a more qualified, mature, and seasoned professional. As I worked in this professional environment over the span of six months, I was furnished with a plethora of skills. My personal and professional development were nurtured as I gleaned from the professionals and recognized the expectations of a professional work environment. I had the firsthand experience of seeing how other mature professionals conducted themselves in the workplace. The skills gained contributed to my readiness and preparedness for college, career, and adulthood. As a teacher's assistant, I was expected to conform to the professional code of ethics for teachers which directly informed my relational capacity with students, colleagues, and parents. In addition, I recognized that an important tenet of being a professional was punctuality. A time sheet was required; signing in and out kept me in compliance with work hours. As time progressed, I was entrusted with small responsibilities in the classroom, and soon after around the school. With said responsibilities, preparation and organization were needed to effectively execute the assigned tasks with excellence. I also learned to work as a team player in substituting for absent teachers and helping in fundraising activities. In addition, the dress policy guidelines motivated me to dress for success in the workplace and by extension wherever I go. This requirement showed me that my attire was imperative to my job because it served as a form of non-verbal communication. Over time I realized that my attire speaks before I do, whenever I enter a room.

Along with non-verbal communication, my verbal and written communication skills improved as there was ongoing interaction with members of staff. As a trainee, I was not given a full salary; alternatively, I was paid a monthly stipend. Inevitably, learning to budget ensued since I had small expenses like paying for my taxi, lunch, savings, and giving contributions to the household. Strong accountability ensured my compliance with the expectations of the workplace, as well as with the National Youth Service Program. There were non-negotiable check-ins with the directors of the program, where my time sheets were validated to confirm my attendance, and punctuality; these determined my pay.

Ultimately, my enrollment in the National Youth Service Program initiated a work ethic that prepared me for college and subsequently reflects in my career today. It was during my tenure in the program that I got inspired to become an educator. Eventually, I applied for teachers' college, the Mico University College, and was accepted. Moreover, as a successful participant of the program, I was granted financial assistance toward my college tuition.

The day I got accepted to the Mico, I missed the call. I was still a participant in the National Youth Service Program and so my cell phone was silent and perhaps, I was busy with assigned tasks. I eventually got around to my phone and realized that there was a missed call and voice mail. I immediately retrieved the voice mail and realized that a representative from the college had left a message. In the message, I was informed that I was accepted into the science program at the Mico. I was elated, smiling from ear to ear. I relayed the good news to my supervisors, and we were all in celebration. Shortly after, I informed my parents, and we celebrated once again. Acceptance to college propelled a country girl from Trelawny to living in the big city of Kingston. In the blink of an eye, my parents and I were on the journey of dropping me off at college. As my parents prepared to say their good-byes, both wished me well and provided me with sage advice. I can remember a clarion encouragement from my father; he said. "Make sure you go to the Mico and shine." I held on to those words so deep in my heart and have never let them go.

As a freshman in college, it was my first time being away from my family. The environment was new. I had no friends and was far from home. Everything was unfamiliar and I became homesick. Thank God my mother was just a phone call away, as she offered me the needed support. The seniors found pleasure in hazing the freshmen during the orientation period. They had us up by 5 a.m. for exercise, where we sang call and response cadences as we made several laps around the campus. As time progressed, I adjusted to college life in finding my way around campus, meeting friends, going to classes and completing required course work. I also immersed myself in extracurricular activities such as the college band, choir, and even completed electives in keyboard and choir. As I went through the rigorous process of sitting through lectures, prepared for presentations, and completed assignments, I developed and honed my skills as a practitioner of pedagogy. It was in college that I fell in love with writing. Though I majored in biology and minored in chemistry, I felt passion when I wrote those papers for my philosophical and pedagogical courses. Additionally, my love for music deepened as I would listen to music while getting assignments done.

The benefits of going to college are not limited to scholastic achievements. College experience aids in the holistic development of the individual to operate professionally, personally, and socially. Along the way I developed life skills, met lifelong friends, and learned budgeting, work ethic, determination, and soft skills. The choices I made in college contributed to how my life turned out. I had the responsibility of cooking, managing my time, personal, and social life while pursuing my scholastic endeavors. Working collaboratively in college was inevitable. Many of our assignments had a teamwork component. As a team we had to brainstorm, research, strategize, and develop effective methods of executing the assignment. On the day of presentation, the group certainly demonstrated that we understood the assignment. Going to college and persevering until the end brewed grit and consistency as I worked assiduously to meet expectations. The experience also taught me that accomplishing our goals requires meeting deadlines and making prior preparations, which were realized as I prepared for presentations and sat exams. I will never forget a plaque mounted in our study room in college; it stated P.R.E.P Preparation. Reaps. Excellent. Performance. This will forever be embedded in the corner of my mind. Preparation is the work done backstage that makes whatever we do a success. With that said, during my second year of college I was awarded a science scholarship that would span three years. The terms of the scholarship required that at least a 'B' average was maintained and that after graduation, I would serve at least three years as an educator with the Ministry of Education. With gratitude and commitment, I fulfilled my end of the bargain.

College was a cushion between me and the world. I had the opportunity to have a gradual release into life as an independent adult and a professional. I had a chance at budgeting before I had deductions like taxes, insurances, car notes etc. It was not easy getting through college financially even though I had a scholarship for tuition. I learnt to budget the allowance my father would send faithfully each week, which dissuaded the mismanagement of my finances very early. Gradual release into the professional space occurred through various practicum experiences. As a practicing educator, I was assigned to several schools during my tenure at different intervals of my college career. This gave me firsthand experience with procedures, policies, and protocols of operating in the arena of education. At the end of my studies, I achieved a bachelor's degree in education, with a major in biology and a minor in chemistry, with honors. As a new graduate, fresh out of college, I was ready to wet my feet as a professional supported by my pedagogical acumen. This detour disguised as a wrong turn has impacted my life tremendously. The unsuspecting fruit of this detour was a gateway—a ticket on reserve for almost 10 years down the line.

> *"Hope deferred makes the heart sick, but a dream fulfilled is a tree of life."*
>
> Proverbs 13:12 (NLT)

Chapter 5

———∞———

Sleeping with the Enemy

Amazing grace how sweet the sound
that saved a wretch like me!
I once was lost, but now am found,
was blind, but now I see.

-John Newton

Frankie Lymon and the Teenagers released the song "Why Do Fools Fall in Love" in 1956. Why did I fall in love? In 2012 I fell in love with Keith, a guy I shared a few classes with throughout college. We started out in a platonic relationship for about two years where we had lunch together with mutual friends and engaged in small talk here and there. It was my third year of college when I found myself engrossed in a relationship with Keith. Keith was enrolled in the industrial technology program where he majored in electrical technology. On the other hand, I was enrolled in the natural science education program, where I majored in biology. Keith had always appeared to be a calm and helpful individual who would assist anyone, particularly with technological issues. If anyone had a problem with their laptops or any other device, Keith was the go-to person. I admired these attributes I saw in Keith and would even ask him for assistance with computer issues of my own.

Our relationship started off well, it would seem, with laughter, kind gestures, spending countless hours together, and communicating over the phone. They say love is blind, and I sure did fall into this trap. I can clearly remember one day during our relationship at college we had a disagreement. I wanted to excuse myself from Keith's presence, but he would not allow me to. He used the advantage of his strength and muscles to pull me by the arm, followed by a slap on my arm that left the impressions of his fingerprints on my skin. I was upset, but I could not free myself from him. I knew what he did was unacceptable, but I ignored that red flag for the sake of love and to continue our relationship. After all, I thought he was the man I would marry, ride off into the sunset with, and later have children with. Prior to my relationship with Keith, I took salsa dance classes. However, once Keith and I got together, he opposed my dance classes. He expressed that he did not like me taking the classes and wanted me to stop. Again, I ignored this red flag of control and manipulation. Soon after, salsa dancing became a thing of the past. During our college years I also heard rumors that he was seeing this other girl from a different program. I completely ignored the rumors because in my mind, people will talk and are always trying to break up relationships. Right? Being naive to his subtle abuse and alleged relationship, I was headed down a dangerous path. Our relationship continued until we both completed the fourth year of our degree programs.

Our college years came to an end, and it was now summer. Keith had gotten summer employment overseas, and I did not. I was so focused on finding employment for the upcoming school year in September. So, every Sunday I purchased the newspaper and checked vacancies for science teachers. I was also checking vacancies for Keith. I went to countless interviews with hopes of landing employment. I would even send out applications to schools that did not have an ad in the newspaper. Surprisingly, I was called for an interview by one of the schools that did not have an ad in the paper and yes, I got the job. When my employment was confirmed, it was the last weekend right before the school year started. Whew, I was relieved to be finally employed.

I started my teaching career at an all-girls high school where I taught science. Keith was still overseas and so I continued to search for vacancies for him. We still maintained our communication over the phone. One night during our conversation, Keith said that he wanted us to move in together when he returned to Jamaica. I hesitated and said, "I don't think I am ready for us to live together." Given that I was resisting this conversation, Keith started saying things like I was not serious about the relationship. He made it seem like I did not value our relationship and gave a false sense of urgency that we needed to live together. Throughout the conversation I was coerced by Keith to move in with him. This guilt trip made me succumb to his persuasion. By the end of the conversation, I agreed with him that we would move in together when he returned.

One day I got a call from a school that responded to Keith's application; they wanted to interview him. Keith arrived back in

Jamaica in time and attended the interview. Before the day ended, I got a text message from Keith saying that he had gotten the job and that we needed a home. Now, we both have employment in Montego Bay. We found an apartment and moved in together. Everything felt so perfect, and I was happy. We were the perfect example of starting from scratch as we merged our salaries to cover our expenses. We would do grocery shopping together, cook together, budget for our monthly finances while getting settled in our new careers. I thought I was getting ready to start life and eventually a family with the man I loved. In retrospect, my desperate desire to have a redo of having a family contributed to my unwise cohabitation with Keith. My decision was influenced by being young, impressionable, and being robbed too early of the support and ambience a family is intended to offer. It was not even three months into us living together that things started to become tragic. Keith, who appeared so benign in the beginning, had become so hostile. It was as though Keith had mutated into a lethal monster behind closed doors. The stories of abuse that will be shared in this chapter are graphic, but it is the truth of my past. We had disagreements that would lead to some type of abuse. On one occasion we had an argument and Keith resorted to biting me. He was a much bigger guy than me so I was easily maneuvered and could hardly fight back. There was another incident where we were in a heated argument and Keith threw his wallet straight at my face. It missed and I laughed. This aggravated Keith, and he pushed me off the bed. I fell and sustained injuries to my head. On another occasion I was dragged by my arm and thrown to the ground. Keith then came on top of me and had both of his hands squeezing my neck. I felt my tongue pushing out from my head. I hardly ever fought back because I was too afraid that he would overpower me. Most of the time during arguments I would try to ignore Keith. That was my defense. I remember, one day as I ignored him and prepared for work, he came over and ripped every paper I was working on.

Keith was adept in masking his manipulation. Whenever disagreements were not solved in Keith's eyes, I could not leave the house, neither could I sleep or attend work. There were several times that I did not attend work because I was locked in the house by Keith. Sometimes I ended up being extremely late for work because Keith would not allow me to leave until he was satisfied with the conclusion of the disagreement. He always wanted me to keep his secrets of the ways he was treating me. I was supposed to remain quiet and suffer in silence. Keith was particularly upset with me for telling my mother what was going on. He stated that he did not want me to share with anyone what was going on, yet every time I said it was over he would become violent. Keith hardly ever wanted me to spend time with my family. On occasions where I would leave to spend time with my family, Keith's disposition would change to an attitude of vexation and disapproval. This was simply another way he was camouflaging his manipulation. Keith was famous for being oblivious to the ways he treated me, pretending as though he was completely unaware of all the things he did. He made me seem delusional whenever we were attempting to have conversations after a conflict. I would ask why he did this to me; in his response he always found a way to circumvent the truth of his actions. Often, his response would be that he did not know what I am talking about. All along it was a tactic of his manipulation.

In *Me My Mine*, Bishop RC Blakes Jr. writes:

The covert narcissist is incredible at playing mind games. Their specialty is knowing how to make others feel bad. They twist your words into knots and make you believe you did it to yourself. The covert narcissist creates confusion in your life, and you can't always tell where it is coming from. They have a way of tormenting your mind. They cause you to self-doubt, second guess, accuse others and self-condemn.[1]

1 RC Blakes, Jr., *Me My Mine* (2023).55

Keith became so overbearing that he even wanted to show up at social events at my workplace. I remember it was teachers' appreciation day and our staff was treated to a day at a hotel. Keith was highly motivated to show up unannounced. Thank God he did not. During a random conversation, Keith shared that he preferred living in our former studio apartment in comparison to our current one-bedroom apartment. He said that he was no longer able to see me all the time in our one bedroom, whereas in our studio apartment he could. At that time, I could not see that Keith was being obsessive, wanting to hover and keep tabs on my every move. Keith also had deceitful tendencies, which further confirms his manipulation. He intentionally omitted pertinent facts about his life for almost two years into our relationship. I already knew that he had a daughter. Now, two years into the relationship he told me that there was another woman who claimed that he was the father of her son. He never denounced the allegations but never took the initiative to resolve this issue. Additionally, Keith was dishonest about his faith. In the early stages of our relationship, I asked him if he saw himself going back to the church. Keith said that he had been telling himself that he should get back to the church, but he just had not gotten around to it. Years into the relationship, through conversations surrounding the Christian faith, Keith told me that he did not believe in God.

Our conflicts intensified and became more frequent. Keith was a violent man to the point where he destroyed my cellphone by throwing it at the wall during an argument. Whenever arguments escalated, I would say it would be better for us to break up and go our separate ways. This would result in Keith doing even more dark things to me. For instance, I remember one time when I said to him that we need to go our separate ways, Keith tore off my clothes saying if I think I 'm going to shame and embarrass him to go back home to his parents. As he tore off my clothes, he started to drag me towards the door to push me outside of our apartment. I grabbed onto the doorjamb with both of my hands as he pulled my legs towards outside. Out of desperation I yelled, "'I'll stay! I'll stay! I'll do whatever you want!" I burst out bawling as tears flowed down my face. I guess my desperate cry made Keith feel reassured that I no longer wanted to leave and so he stopped pulling me outside.

In other instances of me saying I wanted to leave, Keith would unpack several cords and unravel them leaving them on the kitchen counter. He never said anything but just had them there as I sat in silence. Another episode of abuse occurred because I wanted to leave. Keith boiled water on the stove. He took the pot with the boiling water and tried to pour it on me, but I managed to fight and talk my way out. It seemed like after that talk, he still was not convinced that I would stay. So, Keith turned on the stove again, he grabbed me and started to push my face toward the burner. I could see all the hot, orange, coiled rings starring me right back in the face. I fought and resisted as much as I could. He pushed and I kept fighting back with every strength that I had. I cried and cried some more. I thought my heart would fail because I felt like I could not breathe. I was surprised that I did not pass out. I was in immense panic and shock. I thought that this was the end as I trembled with terror. I was so traumatized and even Keith started to tell me to calm down and as he refrained from pushing my face in the burner.

Even after all this I still stayed in the relationship. It was just a matter of time before we had another heated argument. Keith vacillated between violence and manipulation. He started to force me to post pictures of him on my social media, which I refused to do. Keith was not only abusive, but he was also a cheater. Later, I found out that Keith was indeed cheating with the girl from college I had heard about. I found all the evidence on his laptop of sexually explicit photos. He was still communicating with her, and they had slept together in college. All this happened in less than a year of us living together.

By this time, we had moved into our second apartment. Keith said that he had now discontinued all communication with the girl from college. I found out that he did not, and even more details about the relationship he had with this girl were revealed. I found out about their sexual adventures. I knew it was time to leave, so I burnt any picture I had of us. I knew I could not let Keith know that I was planning to leave the relationship. I had learnt that I could not have a conversation about leaving with Keith, otherwise abuse would result. One Sunday I decided that I would go to church because I was so overwhelmed and frustrated. It was my first time going to this church, so nobody knew me. At some point in the message the preacher said, "Sometimes you must just leave!" He pressed on to say, "You may have to leave behind everything, be it furniture etc." I was shocked when I heard this. It was like God had sent a message my way. Eventually, I decided to leave on my own terms without telling Keith my intentions. On the day I decided to leave I packed my things and charted a taxi while Keith was at work. I called my mom and told her I was coming home. I cried again and again. It was customary for Keith and me to talk on the phone until he got home from work. As he was about to enter the apartment I burst into tears as he opened the door and realized I was gone. All I heard Keith saying was "You left!" Keith started to cry and said he was going to kill himself and that I needed to come back. Deep down I felt like I wanted to go back. While on the phone he started to tell me how he was going to try and kill himself, particularly to hang himself. I guess he was trying to instill fear in me. He kept convincing me that I needed to come back. This was simply Keith's way of manipulating me to move back in with him, but I did not recognize it at the time. Later, I gave my mother a very superficial explanation of what was happening and why I had left. My mother wanted to have a conversation with Keith, and he agreed. After the talk with my mother, I decided to move back in with him. Crazy, right? When I got back to our apartment, I saw a rope hanging from a post with a building block under the rope. Upon going inside, the apartment was ruined, and my furniture had been destroyed. Broken glasses were everywhere. During previous arguments Keith had threatened to destroy the furniture, but now it was a reality.

When I moved back in, I thought things would improve; instead, things escalated and became more life threatening. During disputes Keith started to ask me if I knew about crimes of passion. In other instances of me wanting to leave he told me that if I still wanted to be around, I would have to get rid of him. I was anxious, nervous, and wanted a way out. Numerous times in the shower I cried my eyes out, begging God to take Keith out of my life. I had no idea how it would happen because I was concerned about my safety and the logistics of relocating and keeping my job.

"See, Lord. how distressed I am! I am in torment within, and in my heart, I am disturbed, for I have been most rebellious. Outside, the sword bereaves; inside, there is only death."

Lamentations 1:20 (NIV)

Months passed and we now moved to our third apartment. What was I thinking right? Did things start to change? Absolutely not. We were still having ongoing fallouts. Soon after, there was another altercation surrounding the same girl from college. Keith had a seminar in Kingston which required him to be away for several days. I had no suspicions and was quite comfortable with him being away. Keith left and I was at home by myself. While at home I heard a text message coming in on a phone that Keith seldom used. Of course I checked to see who it was. It was the same girl from college sending him a text message about what time they were planning to meet up while at the seminar. After exchanging a few messages, I realized what exactly was going on. They both met at the seminar and who knows what really went down after that. Having gathered enough information, I contacted Keith and told him that I knew what was going on with him and that girl. I told him that I was leaving, and I did. I packed my suitcases for the second time and went to my mother's. Keith reached out to me several times convincing, me that I needed to come back. Guess what I did. I moved right back in. I suggested to Keith that we should seek counseling to help us work out our problems. He agreed that we would pursue counseling.

Upon moving back with him I deliberately did not mention anything about getting enrolled in counselling sessions. As one could imagine, Keith did not initiate any action in getting our counselling sessions started. Inevitably, as time progressed nothing changed in our relationship, and we continued having our disagreements. I believe Keith used his agreement to attend counseling as an incentive to make me think things were about to change. The threats never stopped. I can recall one night as I cried, he shouted "Shut up!" He grabbed the extension cord and asked if I wanted something to cry about. Keith's abuse was not limited to physical abuse; there were several instances where expletives were hurled at me. He would always belittle me regarding my hair and mockingly cackled in laughter whenever I shared my aspirations, followed by a pat of pity on my back. There was a lack of affirmation and celebration. With all this, Keith still wanted my love, attention, and affection. He even became upset if I did not oblige. Keith was physically, verbally, and emotionally abusive. He was so unconscionable and demanded that I accepted his promiscuous living. He expected me to stay with him even though he had slept with another woman and did not treat me well. Keith would show his abuse in another way. If he wanted to communicate his disapproval about a situation, he would say, "Do you want me to give you one of those hugs?" He would "hug" and squeeze me so hard that I would literally feel like my ribs were about to break. He would respond with laughter or a chuckle of satisfaction.

Desperate times call for desperate measures. I was in a high-risk situation. Things were horrific and I needed to get out. With this bleak reality, I knew I had to extricate myself from this relationship once and for all. We were living above the ground floor of our apartment building. It was between one and three in the morning when Keith opened all the doors that led outside the apartment and was behaving haphazardly. I sat in silence because I was afraid of what he might do. I knew it was time to go. The next conflict was the straw that broke the camel's back. During this argument Keith took a long kitchen knife and slapped me on my leg. I could feel the pain tingling through my leg. He then held the knife to my face and then to my eyes. At this point the knife was a few millimeters away from my eyes. I had to use my hands to hold and push against the knife, but he kept pushing the knife towards my eyes. I gripped the knife as it sank into the flesh of my hands. Keith eventually stopped and I could see the imprint of the knife in my hand. Not being satisfied, Keith got electrical paraphernalia, disconnected wires and exposed the uninsulated ends. He made connections to an electrical socket and started trying to electrocute me. Remember, Keith's bachelor's was a major in electrical technology, so he knew exactly what he was doing. I was frantically jumping and screaming as he told me to shut up! He continued to try and electrocute me but for some reason it did not work. I now know this was the Lord protecting me. Isaiah 54:17 declares that no weapon that is formed against us will prosper. This word stood true on that night even though I did not recognize it then. I could have lost my eyes, moreover, my life in being stabbed to death or being electrocuted. In this precarious moment I knew without a doubt I needed to run for my life.

Living in turmoil, my stress levels were at an all-time high. I repeatedly made the wrong decision of going back to Keith and staying in the relationship. Later, I found that he had bugged my cellphone and was viewing every activity on my phone. In my opinion, Keith got comfortable and complacent with his behavior because he was confident that I would never leave. Keith realized that he could continue to get away with his behavior without consequences. After all, I would always run right back into the relationship with him even when my life and safety were in jeopardy.

It was now December 2016, and one of my greatest inconvenient choices became my way of escape. My only escape was to flee to my father without ever looking back. I had a plan and was ready to execute it. During the Christmas break, Keith and I planned to visit our own parents separately. Yes, this was my window of escape. So, I went to my father and briefly explained what was going on and told him I needed to spend some time with him. I told him I needed to move out immediately. Without hesitation my father immediately agreed, and I was able to move my furniture and other items out the very next day. Once I made the move, I remember my sister saying to me, "No turning back." She said this because she knew that I had previously moved out several times but would always go back to Keith. Moving back to my father's house had a dual benefit because my safety was sure, but it also provided the perfect opportunity for the relationship to be mended between me and my father. Being safely out of the apartment, I contacted Keith and told him that I had moved out for good this time. Keith started crying and was asking all sorts of questions. He asked if there was someone else and was convinced that someone encouraged me to move out. For the entire holiday my phone was bombarded with incessant phone calls and text messages from Keith, his friends, and his mother. Keith expressed that he was willing to work on the relationship even from a distance, but I had no intentions of ever going back. I changed my number with hopes that this was really the end. But was it? I went to the police station and gave a formal complaint. The authorities called Keith and gave him a stern warning that he needed to stay away from me and that if anything happened to me, he would be the first person of interest.

In my mind I was finally out of harm's way, but I knew it was an uphill climb to regain my confidence, self-esteem, and mental health. I felt free and liberated now that I was no longer sleeping pillow to pillow with an abuser. Yet, there was still a lingering dark cloud, because I knew Keith too well. I knew Keith would strike again. My greatest fear was that Keith would secretly wait for me at the bus stop. To get to work, I had to travel across parishes daily and I relied on public transportation.

It was now the new year, January 2017, and it was time for school to resume. As I got ready for the first day of work in the new year Keith kept calling my old number over and over. I ignored all the calls. I made it to work without a sign of Keith that morning. Unfortunately, what lay ahead was brutal and gruesome. If this was a movie, this is where ominous music would begin to play. After work, I headed towards the bus stop to get back home. When Keith and I lived together he could barely make it home before sunset. However, on this day it was obvious that he had left work promptly because he was already lurking at the bus stop waiting for me to arrive. As I stood there, I saw Keith across the other side of the road. At that moment I realized my greatest fear became a reality. He quickly made his way across and with the twinkling of an eye Keith was standing right next to me. I was worried, anxious, and my heart palpitated. Keith started to talk to me, but I constantly ignored him. I could see people passing by looking on, but everyone continued to mind their own business. Before I knew it, Keith started to drag me away from the bus stop and I was now at a park between the beach and the highway. Keith tore off my pantyhose and partially undressed me. He took away my handbag and cellphone. Even though I was crying and told him to stop, he still forced himself on me and threatened to rip off all my clothes to expose me if I did not allow him to have his way. By now it was late, and my father was expecting that I should be home. But I did not have my phone because Keith had taken it. After all that,

Keith was still trying to tell me that I should come back to him. I was adamant that it was over and so Keith started saying he would kill himself by running into vehicles passing on the highway. He made attempts to run into oncoming vehicles but never did. Instead, he resorted to saying that he should climb on one of the high-rise buildings and jump off.

I managed to make it away from the park and back to the bus stop. Keith gave me back my handbag but searched through my cellphone as he questioned me about my contacts. I had a new phone that was still in my bag that Keith did not know about. Unknowingly, as we stood at the bus stop the new phone in my handbag happened to open the line to one of the incoming calls from my family. This provided the opportunity for them to hear surrounding conversations that revealed my location. They realized I was trapped in Montego Bay. My father's wife later told me that when my father recognized I was not coming home he became infuriated. He told her he had a feeling that Keith had held me captive in Montego Bay. She added that my dad got dressed furiously and told his wife that he was heading off to Montego Bay in search of me. My dad called one of his cousins for backup to come and rescue me. However, the mission was aborted when I finally managed to call my father and let him know I was on a bus heading home. As a result, my father discontinued his journey and gave his cousin the update. We often hear of a mother's intuition. Conversely, on this night my father's intuition was triggered, which propelled him to set off to Montego Bay in search for me.

So back to the bus stop. Keith finally gave me back my phone and I had a million missed calls. He eventually allowed me to get on a bus. I frantically got on a bus, in shock from all the eventualities of the night. I never thought I would see the end of that night. It appears Keith started to have second thoughts about letting me go. So, he jumped onto the step of the bus with efforts of getting to me. As the bus drove off Keith was forced to jump from the steps because the bus was too fast, and the door shut on him. With my heart raging I looked back as the bus departed and I could no longer see Keith. This moment perfectly describes a narrow escape. I immediately called my father and told him I was on a bus heading home. He discontinued his journey and waited for me until the bus arrived at the final stop. During the journey home Keith kept calling but I never answered. On the night of the incident my mother told me she kept calling Keith's phone, but he refused to answer. He eventually answered and she inquired about my whereabouts. Keith responded quite casually that he had merely seen me and spoke as though nothing happened that night.

Upon meeting with my father, I told him the whole story. Keith kept calling my phone and my father asked aggressively, "Is that him?" I said yes.

My father said, "Let me talk to him." So, I gave my phone to my dad. My dad exclaimed, "Leave my daughter alone!"

I could hear the whimper of Keith's voice responding, saying, "Yes, sir." My father continued to speak to him harshly and all I could hear from Keith was "Yes, sir, yes, sir." After hanging up, my father turned to me and said, "You must make another report at the police station." I sank inside because it was an embarrassing and traumatizing experience and all I wanted to do was hide. I had to give a full detailed report to the police of all the events that night. So, I gave the report to the police and was taken to the hospital to undergo the full procedures for rape victims. My father and I left the hospital at approximately 3 a.m. I would never have imagined that morning as I got ready for work that my day would end in such tragedy. The harassment and sexual exploitation leading to making a police report and undergoing medical evaluation as a victim of sexual assault was unimaginable. Due to the incident, I was overloaded with medications for several weeks and was placed on leave of absence from work. Can you imagine spending my birthday in bed nauseated by all these medications? To say the least it was debilitating. Upon reflection, if it was not for my father, I could have ended up pregnant that night or left with an untreated STD. This could have been my reality, because all I wanted to do was hide some place far away and never tell. If I had forgone going to the police, I would not have been transferred to the hospital where I received the necessary medical treatment for being sexually assaulted.

My leave ended and I was terrified to return to work. I happened to bump into Keith twice after returning to work. I believe he was stalking me. On one occasion he got onto the bus as we waited for departure, trying to convince me to come back to him. I hardly responded and ignored him. He eventually left the bus. That was the last day I ever saw Keith because I started taking alternative bus routes. According to Centers for Disease Control and prevention, approximately 41% of women have experienced contact sexual violence, physical violence, and/or stalking by an intimate partner.

https://www.cdc.gov/violenceprevention/
intimatepartnerviolence/fastfact.html

I eventually got my driver's license and promptly transitioned from public transportation. I give immense gratitude to God for this breakthrough. Ever since this ordeal with Keith, going to Montego Bay was never the same. Whenever I was in the city, I frequently looked over my shoulder, wondering if Keith was lurking nearby. Shortly after, depression started to slowly creep in since I was no longer in fight or flight mode. I finally got the chance to truly process the silent trauma I was enduring due to the agony of living with Keith. The numbness started to subside, and I began to feel the real pain of my story. I was drowning in despair, which led to me plunging into depression. My self-esteem, identity, and confidence had plummeted. I was swamped with feelings of hopelessness, and defeat dominated my mind. As I plunged further into depression, I felt worthless, useless and my life seemed purposeless. Being so low in spirit, mind and body, all I could see were the ashes of my self-esteem, confidence, and self-worth.

Persistent? Yes, that was Keith. He struck again. Since he could no longer get ahold of me, he decided to attack my character. He undoubtably cast an aspersion on me as he made me out to be the villain in the eyes of his friends and family. I was the one who held on in this struggling love and kept going back time after time. Yet I was the villain. They repeatedly asked me if there was someone else. Keith made it seem as though I had used him. For what? One could ask. We lived together, shared expenses, and he was guilty of the mismanagement of our finances. We had a joint bank account, and upon leaving I did not even withdraw a dollar. I was done. I even brought it to his attention that he should check the account and see that I had not touched it. I wanted to make it obvious that I wanted nothing to do with him. I made a clarion statement to him that he should withdraw all the money, so that I would not have any access to it. He sure did make the transfer, leaving the account spanking clean. I was okay with it because I just wanted him to know that I was done. That still was not enough for Keith. Can you believe he wanted me to repay him for the money he spent during our relationship? He went to the extent of sending me a document requiring me to pledge that I would pay money over to him.

Throughout this chapter of my life, I spent most of my days worried in fear with anxiety. I really cannot fathom how I survived those years. The trauma was real, piercing, inhumane, and exhausting. It was a period of my life when I never thought I would see the break of day. Looking back at the relationship, I realized I was always touched sexually but never touched affectionately. I realized that Keith never truly loved me. He was so insensitive even when I was sick. Keith would sit and watch me suffer without offering any assistance. My constant thoughts were that I needed to get out, but I never know how I would. I felt like I was caught in an everlasting trap. I mustered up the courage and reached out to my father at the stroke of that final life-threatening encounter with Keith. I am grateful that my father responded with immense urgency when I expressed to him what was going on. It is amazing that for so long I worried with fear and anxiety about how I would safely get out of the relationship with Keith. This worry and anxiety were simple mental shackles that helped to keep me trapped. These shackles seemed to have disappeared into thin air because of the way my father handled the situation. My father made it a seamless transition of moving out, where all my concerns were taken care of and more.

The moral of the story is to not allow fear, anxiety, or the unknown to prevent us from extricating ourselves from poisoning circumstances. I would also advise everyone to trust their instincts. I had been with Keith for so long that I understood the pattern of his proclivities. Something deep down told me that he would be at the bus stop that afternoon. I made the mistake of discounting my instinct and walked right into Keith's conspiracy.

I would tell my younger self that there is a rocky journey ahead, but you will become the woman you are through the turbulent experiences of life. I would also say to her that these experiences are all journeys that constitute your unique journey of life. Additionally, I would caution her that abusers sometimes masquerade themselves as being cool, calm, and collected. Keith perfectly epitomized a wolf in sheep's clothing, because no one would tell that he was a closet abuser. After all, he was the cool computer guy, with a bachelor's in electrical technology, dressed in tailored pants, long sleeved shirt, a tie, and his attaché case heading out to work.

In conclusion, Keith got away scot free. My case slid through the cracks of the justice system. An odious crime went unpunished. He was never arrested nor charged. I made countless trips back and forth to the police station. Every time I went it was a new officer who was oblivious to my case. Therefore, I had to retell and relive the trauma each time. On each occasion I was given a different explanation as to why the case was not going forward. I was told that the crime occurred outside of their jurisdiction and so they could not act. I was assured that the report would have been transferred to the jurisdiction in which it happened. Consequently, I was directed to the Center for Investigation of Sexual Offences and Child Abuse (CISOCA) at the Mount Salem Police Station in Montego Bay. I went and inquired about my case, and nobody was aware of it. I was devastated. Mentally, I felt like I was left in ruins since there seemed to be an impasse to my case. Following that I made various trips back to the police station where I made the original report and made more enquiries. I even had to redo the original report. Even after all that, justice was never served. I grew weary and frustrated from all these trips to the police station and so my visits got fewer and fewer until I stopped all together. Over time, I have grown to embrace Romans 12:19 NLT "Dear friends, never take revenge. Leave that to the righteous anger of God. For the Scriptures say, 'I will take revenge; I will pay them back,' says the Lord."

Many victims of domestic abuse have not survived to tell their stories. Some victims of domestic abuse are still grappling with silent traumas, muffled by their abuser. I have shared my story for those without the courage to verbalize their untold stories. I shared for those who are too ashamed, embarrassed, and hide their stories in their hearts. I shared for those behind bars with untold stories. Moreover, I have shared my story as a representation of all those who never survived. Many times, the stories of domestic abuse are posthumously shared. However, since I am a survivor, I will be a voice for domestic violence endured by women. In *Woman Thou art Loosed,* Bishop T.D. Jakes writes about Tamar, a woman found in 2 Samuel 13:1-21. He described Tamar as a survivor of sexual exploitation at the hands of her brother. Jakes writes,

The name Tamar means "palm tree." Tamar is a survivor. She stands in summer and spring. She even faces fall with leaves when other trees lose theirs. She still stands. When the cold blight of winter stands in her face, she withstands the chilly winds and remains green throughout the winter. Tamar is a survivor. You are a survivor. Through hard times God has granted you the tenacity to endure stresses and strains.[2]

Jakes continues:

Tamar was victimized brutally, yet she survived. There is hope for victims. There is no need to feel weak when one has Jesus Christ. His power is enough to bring about the kinds of changes that will set you free. He is calling, through the work of the Holy Spirit, for you to be set free.[3]

In an article written by the World Health Organization, it emphasizes that worldwide, many women have suffered physical and/ or sexual violence from their partner in their lifetime. WHO writes,

Estimates published by WHO indicate that globally about 1 in 3 (30%) of women worldwide have been subjected to either physical and/or sexual intimate partner violence or non-partner sexual violence in their lifetime.

Most of this violence is intimate partner violence. Worldwide, almost one third (27%) of women aged 15-49 years who have been in a relationship report that they have been subjected to some form of physical and/or sexual violence by their intimate partner. Violence can negatively affect women's physical, mental, sexual, and reproductive health...

---

2 *Bishop T. D. Jakes, Woman Thou art Loosed* (1993), 73.

3 Jakes, *Woman Thou art Loosed,* 83.

WHO continues,

Globally as many as 38% of all murders of women are committed by intimate partners. In addition to intimate partner violence, globally 6% of women report having been sexually assaulted by someone other than a partner, although data for non-partner sexual violence are more limited. Intimate partner and sexual violence are mostly perpetrated by men against women.

Ultimately, I can share my story because I have been redeemed by the endless love of God. God's love and redemption gave me the empowerment to be bold and courageous enough to share my story. I share from the standpoint of freedom, wholeness and a healed heart with a story to tell. Psalm 107: 2 NIV "Let the redeemed of the Lord tell their story—those he redeemed from the hand of the foe." In the next chapter I will share how being redeemed has forever changed my life. The Lord has undoubtably redeemed me from my past and now I have further overcome by the word of my testimony.

Violence against women March 9, 2021
Violence against women (who.int)

Chapter 6

———⸎———

Redeemed

What a friend we have in Jesus,
All our sins and griefs to bear!
What a privilege to carry
Everything to God in prayer!

- George Scriven

Have you ever felt angry with God? I spent a few years being angry with God. I wondered why He allowed that turmoil to happen in my life. I had stopped going to church and kept asking, "God, where were You? Why me?" Eventually, I decided to drag myself to church one Sunday. I chose the very back row of the sanctuary to sit in. I enjoyed the service and felt motivated to continue visiting and so I did. Another Sunday as I sat in the back row of the church, I kept ruminating on the disarray of my life. It just did not make sense to me. I pondered why this story was mine. I did not want to own it. In my mind this is something that no one will ever know because I will never share this story for sure. In my mind I wanted to dispose of this memory like a bag of trash and wave goodbye with hopes of never facing it again. I tried to forget and tried to live as though these memories never existed. It was a memory that I wanted so desperately to get rid of. I hated it so much and frequently asked why I could not just forget it. I needed this chapter to be forever erased from my mind. I wondered why we can't just forget memories like these. It happened, and I know I cannot change the past, but why can't I just forget? That same Sunday, as I sat in the back row in church I had an epiphany. I realized I had a testimony! Even then, I still did not know if, when, or how I would share this story. I still held on to it in my heart; but at least I felt that there was significance and power in my experience.

As I continued going to church, I rededicated my life to Christ. When I was younger, I grew up in the Pentecostal church. However, I never understood what it meant to have a real relationship of walking in step with the principles of Christ. Being rededicated, I made the decision to pursue this commitment to walk with Christ. I was already baptized, so my next steps were to repent and start my Christian journey of abiding in Christ so He could abide in me. I started by being devoted to devotionals and becoming a part of my church community. I attended church on Sundays for morning service and Fridays for Young Generation Ministries. I started to meet new people and became active in the church. Eventually, I served as the church secretary, ushered on a few occasions, moderated Sunday services, camp meetings, and even funeral services.

My local church announced that they would be doing the 21-day Daniel fast. Once I heard 21 days of fasting, I immediately made the decision that there's no way I would be participating in this corporate activity. Consequently, I did not give it a second thought. Interestingly, the Saturday evening prior to the beginning of the fast, which was the following Sunday, I felt a great urgency to get prepared for the fast. I felt compelled to go the market and purchase the necessary fruits and vegetables needed for the fast. At the time I could not tell where the impetus came from. That Saturday, without hesitation, I headed straight to the market and purchased the necessary items. In hindsight, it was apparent that I was under the influence of the Holy Spirit. I started the fast with uncertainty, not knowing what to fast about or what to expect. At the end of the fast it was impossible to resort to business as usual. The fast came to an end, but the new lifestyle continued. These 21 days of fasting served as a reset for my life in general. It was the watershed moment in my faith journey that had a lasting impact on my life until today. A new lifestyle was born which made the fast seem like it did not end. My life was drastically changed from the experience. My mind was never the same, and the fast placed me on a path that I could not discontinue. The fast had an unforgettable effect on me and changed the trajectory of my life. The fast served as a door of transition. Having gone through this door, it was unthinkable to ever reverse my steps to the opposite side of it. I had walked through a door of no return. My mind was renewed, and my eyes were propped open. I saw things through a new lens and started a journey—a whole new life with no intentions to cease. It was out of the question to deviate from this path. It was as though I was taken by the hand and guided to stay on this path.

There was no interest, desire, nor craving to return to life before the fast. This change was captivating. I only wanted to find out more and experience the work of God I was reading in the Bible. I was eager to see what else the Bible had to offer. I just wanted more.

There was a call; a voice I could not ignore. This call was like a fish being caught on a fisherman's hook. I was gradually being pulled in by God, without resistance to the pull. On this journey, I saw and learnt hidden truths and secrets in scriptures and dreams. God is still working on me, but I am all in for the journey. Making this decision to follow Christ felt like I arrived at a fork on the highway and had taken a completely different exit from everyone else. I was focused on my path and was not enticed nor concerned by the direction of the other traffic. This focus on my path was sustained because of that hook in my jaw. This was a life journey to an unknown destination, because I did not have the map. I must, however, insert this caveat: there were many times I veered off track due to disappointments and distractions, but that never quenched my desire to continue the journey. I've had to bow low in reverence and repentance multiple times, so I could still hear and follow the voice of the Father. There were times I even felt overwhelmed and condemned when I had fallen. Dealing with feelings of being unworthy to be in the presence of God was not easy. However, God is faithful, forgiving, and full of mercy. He often consoles my heart with reassurance in songs like He did not throw the clay away. God did not give up on me, because He has the product in mind. I made the intentional effort of listening to God's voice because I was determined to walk this path until the very end.

> "Here I am! I stand at the door and knock. If anyone hears my voice and opens the door, I will come in and eat with that person, and they with me."
>
> Revelation 3:20 (NIV)

BROKEN BRICKS STILL BUILD

The 21 days of fasting brought about lifestyle changes that I will never trade for anything. During this time, I read 1st and 2nd Samuel, binge-watched sermons, spent time in fellowship with God through prayer, sought God intentionally, and tuned to worship music. I allowed the words of the worship songs to pierce deep within and minster to my soul. As I listened to the songs and watched worship videos tears uncontrollably flowed from my eyes. I never understood what was happening to me, but I guess it was a language or response of being in the presence of the Lord. Having gone through the 21 days of fasting, I recognized that fasting is not so much about staying away from food. Fasting was a retreat for me because I had the opportunity to distance myself from all the distractions and stresses of life. I began to focus on God by asking questions with the anticipation to receive answers. I started to learn scriptures, and the truths from these texts permanently marked my heart forever. I gained direction for my life and patterns were forever changed. I came out of the 21 days of fasting transformed and a new version of myself emerged. It felt like something unlocked that birthed this transformation in me. Fasting—I highly recommend it.

Since I grew up in the Pentecostal church, it was inevitable to witness people speaking in tongues. However, I could not relate to this experience. I have always heard about the power one receives after being filled with the Holy Spirit. Certainly, I desperately wanted to receive and experience this power. As I continued my Christian journey, I thought to myself that it seems like only selected individuals would receive the gift of the Holy Spirit. I wondered why I was yet to have this experience. So, I decided to go on three days of fasting in pursuit of being filled with the Holy Spirit. After the three days of fasting, nothing happened. Determined, I went back on three days of fasting again in the following week. Once more, nothing happened. Naturally, I became concerned and discouraged. I asked God what it would take for me to be filled.

Thereafter, I started researching online on how to be filled with Holy Spirt. I had a laser focus and was willing to do whatever was necessary to have this encounter. I stumbled across a video by Creflo Dollar where he spoke about receiving the gift of the Holy Spirit. He spoke about how he started to speak in syllables and then there was a flow of unknown tongues. After I watched this video, I still wondered when and how I would be filled with the Holy Spirit. So, I had now done three days of fasting for two consecutive weeks and I still did not receive the Holy Spirit. It was now Sunday of the third week, and I was still waiting and believing to be filled with the Holy Spirit. I searched my heart to see if something was wrong with me. I went to church during the day, and I still did not get a breakthrough. I left church feeling so disappointed, especially because I once again witnessed other saints speaking in tongues. It was now Sunday night and I tuned into an online service. The preacher began speaking on a scripture that the Lord had been speaking to me about. I broke down in tears. I went to my room and started praying. I told the Lord that He must give me a breakthrough tonight and I will not stop until He fills me with the Holy Ghost. I was on the floor in my room praying and crying, hoping the Lord would grant my request. I even got in my closet and was there travailing with a desperate heart saying, "Lord, just fill me." I was praying for a long period of time and still did not receive the Holy Spirit. So, I left my bedroom and went to the back room of the house. In my mind, I was ready to really cry out and beg the Lord to fill me with Holy Spirit. So, in the back room I kept praying and crying with exhaustion to the Lord. I kept telling the Lord that He must give me a breakthrough tonight. At one point it would seem like I saw Jesus walking away but I said, "No, come back, You must give me a breakthrough tonight." My heart was saying, "Pass me not, oh gentle Savior." I travailed some more and then the moment of truth happened. A syllable came out just like Creflo Dollar said. Then another and another. Then I felt my tongue twisted like I was a baby learning to speak but it was gibberish. The syllables kept coming quickly; clear and more distinct one after the other. Then I said to the Lord, "This is not what I asked for!" Before I knew it, I was speaking in full blown tongues. The day of Pentecost was repeated. In my heart I was screaming yes! Yes! Yes! I was speaking in tongues for over an hour. There was a point where I even found myself singing in tongues. In my mind I was screaming to the devil "You are a liar!" I struggled for so long, thinking that speaking in tongues was only for selected individuals. I spoke in extremely unusual tongues, which is exactly what I asked the Lord for. It was a wonderful experience I would not trade for anything in the world. Praise God! I can testify to my encounter of being truly filled with the Holy Spirit.

The Lord confirmed my encounter that same week during a camp meeting at my local church. The preacher spoke about the story of Jacob, who wrestled with God, saying he would not let Him go until He blessed him. It felt like this story was parallel to the experience I had that night. Just as Jacob wrestled with the Lord, I also fought for a breakthrough. I am marked forever, seeing how the Lord answered my prayers, honored my fasting, and confirmed me wrestling for the breakthrough by means of His word.

"So, we fasted and petitioned our God about this, and he answered our prayer."

Ezra 8:23 (NIV)

So, I was slowly and gradually building my foundation in Christ. I was doing my best to live a life of obedience to the scriptures. However, there was one thing that kept bugging me—the tithe. I had repeated conversations in my mind about tithing. When I did the calculation for 10% of my salary, I said to myself, how can I really give all this money to the church? Little did I know that the Holy

Spirit was tugging at my heart to give Him back a small 10% of what He had given me. Surprisingly, one Sunday as I sat in church and contemplated if I should start to tithe, an usher held out an envelope and asked if I would like a tithing envelope. Without hesitation, I reached out my hands and said "Thank you" as I took the envelope from her. From that day forward I continued to tithe. I never gave out of abundance; I gave out of obedience and sacrifice. After all, I was a schoolteacher. I tithe from my gross salary, sale of my car, tutoring, bonuses, and even tax return. Tithing was not easy at first, but the more I honored this monthly sacrifice, the more I learnt that I was showing gratitude to God for what He has blessed me with. Tithing has taught me to recognize that everything belongs to God and that I own nothing. It also opened my eyes to the fact that God gives, takes and He is in control. Tithing also allowed me to surrender my life to Christ even more, realizing that I am not my own and that I belong to Him. I became more sold out for Christ because now I was leaving my whole life in His hands. God was gracious enough to bless me with an income; who am I to withhold my tithe?

In the final analysis of this chapter, I use one word to describe this part of the journey: Redeemed. Jesus intercepted my tracks and started to show me things I had never seen (Jeremiah 33: 3) and showed me that there is a better way to live life. Jesus showed up and healed my broken heart and stitched up my wounds of low self-esteem and low self-worth. He restored my soul when He corrected my contorted view of myself and dissipated depression and despair from my life. This collision with Christ reignited my hope as the fingers of God directed my eyes to Psalm 27:13. That affirmed me to be confident that I will see the goodness of the Lord in my life. Regardless of my past pain, I am encouraged that I will witness God's goodness in the land of the living. Jesus made the difference because He showed me that it was possible to be relieved from the pit of hopelessness, regret, low self-esteem, and depression. Ever since I allowed God to heal my heart and stitch up my wounds, I have never lived in the chains of hopelessness and despair. I was redeemed because of God's endless love. In the next chapter, I will share how ignorance of God's Word will keep us enslaved in chains of condemnation but the knowledge of who He is gives us the liberty to live out a redeemed life.

I dedicate this chapter to evangelize, to let everyone know that God has redeemed my life and so He will redeem yours too. All you must do is avail yourself of God by opening your heart and allowing Him to show you that doing life with Him is the best way.

Let us break bread together on our knees.
When I fall on my knees with my face to the rising sun,
O Lord, have mercy on me.

Afro-American Spiritual

Chapter 7

—◦◦◦—

Knowledge Liberates

Blessed assurance, Jesus is mine!
Oh, what a foretaste of glory divine!
Heir of salvation, purchase of God,
Born of his Spirit, washed in his blood.

-Fanny Crosby

The words of my high school motto, *Ignorance Enslaves, Knowledge Liberates,* is vastly applicable to the life of the Christian believer. One is held captive by the limits of their experience and the knowledge possessed. Knowledge provides insight and wisdom that is necessary to sustain us on the faith journey. Without knowing who God is, His nature and character, we run the risk of being shortchanged and living in condemnation. Ignorance of who God is will thwart us from experiencing God in His entirety. I believe the knowledge of God is the substratum that tethers us to Him. Growing in Christ absolutely requires gaining substantial knowledge of who God is.

Ignorance to the truth of God had me enslaved to condemnation, worry, and depression for a long time. Even though I had recommitted my life to Christ, I struggled with condemnation. I found myself reflecting on my past and even on the many times I had fallen while on this Christian journey. I felt like I was not holy enough to receive blessings from God. At times I wondered if God would really continue to forgive me over and over. In Romans 8:1, the truth tells us that there is no condemnation for those who are living in accordance with God. This means as a believer there are no accusations owed to me based on my past, because Jesus has liberated me from the sins of yesterday. In Christ I am a new creation, and my old life has passed away; all things are made new (2 Corinthians 5:17). When Jesus died on the cross, He gave me the opportunity to start a fresh through accepting Him as Lord and Savior.

Let us look at the woman who was caught in the act of adultery. In John 8, the religious teachers and Pharisees brought a woman to Jesus who was caught in the act of adultery. Their hope was for her to be stoned and embarrassed in the crowd. The Pharisees failed to recognize that in the presence of the Lord there is no condemnation nor embarrassment. In fact, the Pharisees did this woman a favor by bringing her into the presence of Jesus. Jesus demonstrated His character to the Pharisees and this woman by showing them that in His presence there is no condemnation; instead, there is liberty and correction. At the end of the chapter, the Pharisees left the scene introspecting on their own lives. Jesus then asked the woman if anyone condemned her; she said no. Above all, Jesus said, "Neither do I." He liberated her when He told her to go her way and corrected her by saying, "Moving forward, sin no more."

The knowledge of God's character liberated me when I recognized that I too have daily access to grace and mercy. It is the scheme of the enemy for us to live our lives enslaved to condemnation, but there is access to a fresh start in Christ. I had to acknowledge and accept that once in Christ, each morning as I open my eyes I am already walking in His grace. The veil was torn as Jesus was stretched wide on the cross and said, "It is finished." Therefore, I have access to His grace and so do you. This grace and faithfulness of God allowed me to perceive His patience and everlasting mercies.

> *"It is of the Lord's mercies that we are not consumed, because his compassions fail not. They are new every morning: great is thy faithfulness."*
>
> Lamentations 3:22-23 (KJV)

At some point in our lives all of us become concerned about our future. I found myself worrying about my mine. I constantly asked God, "How will things turn out? How will provisions be made?" I did not have the details nor understood how the events of my life would all culminate to look like His promises. Sometimes I even felt counted out or forgotten. However, my outlook on life started to change when I was enlightened to the truths of God's Word. In Matthew 6, Jesus taught His disciples not to worry about their lives. Jesus brought their attention to the birds and highlighted how they do not sow, reap, or store but the heavenly Father feeds them. In addition, Jesus underscored that our position is superior to the birds. So, if the birds are well taken care of, by default He will supply our needs exceedingly and abundantly. In the text, Jesus makes it obvious to us that He has our lives in His hands and He will certainly take care of us. God orders our steps, and He writes our story. He knows the end from the beginning, and He is the one who puts the pieces of the mosaic together. Whenever fear or worry tries to overwhelm my mind, I remind myself of the truth that God is with me wherever I go and so there is no need to fear. Having this knowledge that God will always be with me liberated me from fear and worry.

"Have I not commanded you? Be strong and courageous. Do not be afraid; do not be discouraged, for the Lord your God will be with you wherever you go."

Joshua 1:9 (NIV)

Struggling with depression was a crippling and exhausting experience. In the next chapter I will further discuss overcoming depression. For years I was enslaved to a state of downheartedness. I ruminated in despair, thinking that no one cared or understood the pain I felt inside. It was a long period of feeling sad and indifferent. Many times, I wondered if I would ever feel lighthearted and exuberant again. I felt like I had lost my smile, and I did not know if I would ever get it back. I wondered who could really relate to what I felt or understand the tears of sorrow that flowed down my cheeks. For so long I lived in ignorance of scriptures that were the perfect medicine for my broken heart. Eventually, through my pursuit I stumbled across the truth that God keeps track of my sorrows, and He even bottles my tears. This reassured me that God has detailed knowledge about the issues of my heart, and He tends to every single wound I have sustained.

"You keep track of all my sorrows. You have collected all my tears in your bottle. You have recorded each one in your book."

Psalm 56:8 (NLT)

Psalm 147:3 further snatched me out of depression when I saw that God heals broken hearts and stitches up wounds. I was honestly taken by surprise when I realized that there was a solution to the turmoil in my heart. I became optimistic that my sorrows could certainly be taken away. My mindset changed due to the knowledge of this scripture and birthed the expectancy that I could get out of this state. Had it not been for this truth, I would still be enslaved to think that there is no one who cares or understands my pain. There is hope for liberty for all of us who have experienced or are still working through depression. None of us are forgotten or will be overlooked, because God has each of our names written on the palms of His hands. According to 1 Peter 5:7, let us cast our cares on Jesus because He cares for us.

"He heals the brokenhearted and binds up their wounds."

Psalm 147: 3 (NIV)

"See, I have written your name on the palms of my hands. Always in my mind is a picture of Jerusalem's walls in ruins."

Isaiah 49:16 (NLT)

Without the knowledge of God, we live without the liberty that is intended for us. We are unable to recognize that there is a new life that salvation offers. Ignorance of the word of God causes one to live beneath God's plan for us. We live in the dark of depression, hopelessness, self-sabotage, and unforgiveness. We live not knowing that the price for our sins is already paid and that in Christ there is no condemnation. Knowledge of God provides us with the defense to endure warfare and resist sin. Without sound knowledge, the enemy can feed our minds with lies that prolong our lives in deception.

For me, I lived with deception for so long that there was no solution to the pain in my broken heart, but I became liberated when I found the truth that God will stitch up my wounds and heal my heart. The more I read, the more I realized I was ignorant and so I kept reading. With the knowledge of God there is sound guidance and principles to live by that will impact the trajectory of our lives. The knowledge of God gives us peace, hope, and changes our perspective and approach to life. It is surprising to see how the knowledge of God can transform our minds and redirect our thought patterns. As I read the scriptures, my faith blossomed. I was so inspired by the stories of how God worked through the lives of different characters and dared to believe that He would work in my life too. Over time, my life was devoted to learning more about God. I believe God rewarded my devotion with revelations of His nature and character.

> *"The Lord confides in those who fear him; he makes his covenant known to them."*

> Psalm 25:14 (NIV)

My heart was ready to have a more in-depth experience of the true essence of God. At this opportune time, I was purposefully positioned to get connected with my mentor—my spiritual mother. With her pastoral care, she fostered my growth and development in Christ. The timing of our connection was impeccable and was the perfect way to segue into a deeper relationship with Christ. My mentor launched different programs for the growth of believers in Christ. During these programs there was accountability for active participation in Bible study. There was an immersion into a Christian community, with regular check ins and discussions where I had the opportunity to ask questions. Throughout this time, I gradually solidified my stance as a believer in Christ. Some of the programs lasted thirty days, while others spanned over three months. It was a sacrifice to participate in these programs, but it was a necessary step to avail myself of a deeper relationship with Christ. It was a time of abiding in Christ so I could glean a copious amount of knowledge about who God is.

Rewards tend to follow the sacrifices we make and often, our greatest gains ensue from those things we deemed insurmountable. During these programs, the participants were required to read prescribed texts and provide personal reports. With these assignments, reading the Bible more and seeking understanding were inevitable. Each day as I read and prepared my reports, there was a new and improved understanding of the scriptures. Some of the scriptures were familiar, while others were completely new. Regardless of the scripture being familiar or not, at the end of each report new knowledge was unveiled. These insights provided more inspiration for me to continue the journey of this Christian walk. The character of Christ gradually became more vivid, and an improved understanding of His mysteries was progressively released. The more knowledge I gained, the more I recognized I was living in ignorance of the truth.

Even at the end of these mentorship programs, I continued to carve out time to explore different books in the Bible. This immersion resulted in my heart being changed and renewed. I was rebuilt into a new individual because my mind was changed from living the same and I started to walk in the freedom that salvation offers. When I allowed the Word of God to minister deep within, I could clearly see how God wanted me to live, be dependent on Him, obey Him and ultimately become like Him. My life slowly and gradually started to reflect the heart of God. It was through the consistent reading of the Word that I saw the true desire the Lord has for us His children. God's number one desire is for us to love Him with all our hearts and then to extend our love to others.

As I delved into the scriptures God's love to me was so undeniably evident. I experienced a love that I never knew before, which taught me how to receive love and how to give love. God's grace and mercy is replete throughout the scriptures and can never be overstated. Whether we have been in church all our lives or not we have heard about God's grace and mercy. The reality is, nothing beats a firsthand experience and that is my testimony. As I reflect on my life, all I can see is an abundance of grace and mercy in times of innocence and even in moments of negligence. It cannot be emphasized enough how having personal Bible study fostered my growth in Christ. The knowledge garnered allowed me to follow Christ from an informed perspective based on the guidance and edification offered. The lessons and hidden truths opened my eyes to the truth that God desires us to live by. My ignorance of the scriptures had limited my awareness of privileges in Christ and the nature of God as *I Am Who I Am.* I recognized the privilege to share my testimony, to live in grace, to start afresh, to be forgiven, to be redeemed and restored. I began to perceive God as the *I Am Who I Am,* the One who is universal for all circumstances. He is the all-inclusive and versatile One who can intervene in any situation. However, how can we access the privileges in Christ if we do not know they exist?

> *"My people are destroyed from lack of knowledge. 'Because you have rejected knowledge, I also reject you as my priests; because you have ignored the law of your God, I also will ignore your children.'"*

Hosea 4:6 (NIV)

The growth I am experiencing in Christ is also attributed to selective choices in media. I absolutely love music and usually appreciate the rhythms and composition of songs. I wondered to myself how could I ever give this up. I questioned if I could ever find gospel music that would captivate me as much as other songs, and so I wrestled with the decision of letting secular music go. There was still a lingering tug in my heart. One day as I sat in my car, I reached into the glove compartment and removed an RnB CD of one of my favorite artists. I broke it in two, saying goodbye with anticipation of what would replace these songs. So, I started searching, not knowing what to expect. I found song after song; flabbergasted and amazed that these songs ever existed. I never imagined that gospel music could ever match the satisfaction that RnB provided. In fact, that is an understatement. The newfound gospel music superseded my taste for RnB; it was a complete overthrow. I sought and I found; I cannot seem to find enough gospel music. Listening to gospel music eventually transcended dancing to the beats as I started listening to the lyrics. The words of these songs completely stole my heart like a lady swooning into the arms of her lover. My heart was arrested and pierced by the messages in these songs, which ushered in tears of worship. There were occasions where as soon as I hit play, I would burst into tears as the songs ministered to me. Overtime, I have built a panoramic playlist ranging from old hymns to contemporary gospel music.

Daily devotionals provided the necessary prompts to read scriptures on a regular basis. These devotionals planted seeds in my heart that stimulated my appetite to seek out the scriptures. There are several scriptures from these devotionals that piqued my interest through the inspirations that ensued. Some resonate with me still today. One of these is "Seek ye first the kingdom of God and His righteousness and all these things will be added to you." The knowledge of this scripture is the reason morning devotionals are priorities in my life. My pursuit led me to watching sermons on YouTube. One sermon led to the next and to the next until several hours elapsed. Being transformed in Christ transcends becoming emotional during sermons, conferences, or reading a book. The application of the knowledge gained after clicking off the sermons and turning the final pages of books accounted for the change in my life. The lasting aftereffect of these encounters progressively shaped me spiritually and personally.

As I continued to mature in my faith, I was asked to speak on different occasions. My first speaking engagement was at the closing of one of our mentorship programs. My mentor extended a second invitation for me to speak at our Sister Supporting Ministries online and sometime later my mother invited me to speak at her church. Our church had an online support group where faith-based content was shared to uplift and edify the believers. From this group, another pastor extended an invitation for me speak at her online event. Eventually, I was asked to prepare weekly meditations for the platform which evolved into the *Teach the Nations; Build the Church* podcast. This responsibility further solidified my growth in the knowledge of Christ, because much time was spent meditating on scriptures and seeking greater understanding. This community offered support from the believers through scriptures shared, encouragement, and their testimonies.

Our brains have the tendency to forget the details of life. Especially after substantial time has passed, we are inclined to lose track of what God has done in our lives. I did not truly appreciate the value of a journal until I started to reflect on past entries. Looking back at these journal entries served as memorials of how God undoubtably worked in my life. In Joshua 4, after the nation of Israel successfully crossed the Jordan River, the Lord gave an instruction to Joshua. He told Joshua to command a man from each of the twelve tribes to take a stone from the middle of the Jordan. This was to serve as a memorial of how God gave the Israelites victory in overcoming the challenge of the Jordan River on their way to the promise. Comparably, revisiting these journal entries brought me to tears so many times when I read my forgotten testimonies. These entries have strengthened my faith and given me hope in times of discouragement and trials. In moments when I was on the brink of forgetting who God is, my journal entries held the knowledge that prevented me from discrediting who God is. Maintaining a journal built my faith and resistance to challenges. These pages house the history of God's hand in the past and it triggers a reflex faith, where I believe God will do it again. Journals serve as more than just an item for retrospection. Over time, I realized that a journal is also a place where revelations are received. This was evident during times when I recorded my dreams. Many times, I could not decipher my dreams and even thought they were nonsensical. However, once I started writing them down, revelations would become clear. Sometimes, the revelations were not instant but were revealed over time.

Learning to give unconditional worship to God is hard, but it was necessary for my growth in Christ. Being a true believer in Christ means offering adoration and worship to God regardless of my current situation. I have realized that the events of life, whether hills or valleys, should not dictate my heart posture to Christ. The story of Job is a clarion example of what it means to offer unconditional worship to God. Job's story postulates that we cannot only worship God in the good times; we should worship Him in the bad times as well. Though Job faced tremendous loss, he still fell to the ground and worshiped God. Even the angels fall on their faces in giving worship and glory to God.

"And all the angels stood round about the throne, and about the elders and the four beasts, and fell before the throne on their faces, and worshipped God,

Saying, Amen: Blessing, and glory, and wisdom, and thanksgiving, and honor, and power, and might, be unto our God for ever and ever. Amen."

Revelation 7:11-12 (KJV)

Every so often we say we are having a good day or a bad day. Consciously, I paused and pondered on these words. Being able to make a connection, I asked myself, how would we know that a day is bad, if we had not experienced a good day? We can perceive bad days because we have the contrasting experience of good days. God in all His wonder blessed us to have a taste of His goodness, through life, health, provisions, joy, peace, etc. While ruminating on this, a heart of gratitude blossomed as I fell in love all over again. The scriptures exhort us to rejoice always and be content in all circumstances. Being content in all circumstances is challenging, for it requires intentional denial of our desires, while hoping that all things are working for our good. Remaining content is an act of submission; trusting that His ways and thoughts are nothing like ours.

"Rejoice in the Lord always: and again I say, Rejoice."

Philippians 4:4 (KJV)

"In every thing give thanks: for this is the will of God in Christ Jesus concerning you."

1 Thessalonians 5:18 (KJV)

Having a church community also provided sound teachings that offered knowledge. The church community is not limited to four walls but extends to online connections. The effectiveness of online church should not be underestimated. There was a season of my spiritual journey where streaming online was my method of connection to the physical church. I was streaming online for Sunday services, watch night services, conferences, and even Wednesday night Bible study. It was during this season of my life that my Christian walk was elevated the most. The impact of the Word was real and was experienced through the crumbs of online church. In Matthew 13:33, the parable of the yeast emphasizes that the Kingdom of Heaven can penetrate to great depths even if only a fraction is experienced.

> "Jesus also used this illustration: 'The Kingdom of Heaven is like the yeast a woman used in making bread. Even though she put only a little yeast in three measures of flour, it permeated every part of the dough.'"

Matthew 13:33 (NLT)

With a firm foundation rooted in the knowledge of Christ, the next step is to bear fruit. Being hearers of the Word only is insufficient for the faith journey; we must be doers of the Word (James 1:22). Galatians 5 explicitly outlines the fruit of Spirit, which is how we truly live a life that reflects Christ. Developing these attributes is an ongoing work in my life as I press toward the mark of the high calling (Philippians 3:13-14). Certainly, navigating life and managing relationships have challenged my ability to live out the fruit of the Spirit. However, it is through these situations that I am being molded to be like Christ. Bearing the fruit of the Spirit is an intentional choice of allowing the Holy Spirit to override impulsive choices.

"But the Holy Spirit produces this kind of fruit in our lives: love, joy, peace, patience, kindness, goodness, faithfulness, gentleness, and self-control. There is no law against these things!"

Galatians 5:22-23 (NLT)

Ignorance Enslaves, Knowledge Liberates!

Chapter 8

———— ✥ ————

Overcoming Depression

I need Thee, oh, I need Thee;
Ev'ry hour I need Thee;
Oh, bless me now, my Savior,
I come to Thee.

-Annie S. Hawks

Tussling through the roller coaster of emotions, I could barely tuck back the sheets to get out of bed. I never had the language to define this experience as depression. My sporadic thoughts vacillated between feelings of worthlessness and happiness. In different moments I felt happy and within seconds there was a sudden crash into feeling purposeless. I have cried so many tears and even cried myself to sleep many nights; I was cried out. God is truly a comforter who is close to the brokenhearted and stitches up our wounds (Psalm 147: 3). There is no hurt He cannot feel and no pain He cannot heal. Ever since my rededication to Christ, God has permanently peeled away these self-destructive thoughts from my mind. That part of my heart is healed to a point of no return. This is evidence that redemption and restoration in Christ do exist. In this chapter I will take you on my journey of overcoming depression.

It was almost five years later, and I was still plagued by the traumatizing memories of my past. I still had dreams of Keith trying to harm me; kill me, chase and stalk me. I was still afraid of him and would become nervous by mere thoughts of him. At times this fear escalated to panic attacks where my heart palpitated with anxiety because of these memories of Keith. Post-traumatic stress disorder (PTSD) had never crossed my mind, but for some reason I kept seeing it on social media. Upon doing a google search, the symptoms for PTSD perfectly mirrored what was happening to me. The more I read, the more I realized that I needed to speak with a therapist.

Shortly after this, I began to speak with a therapist during the Covid-19 pandemic. I shared my story for the very first time as I unfolded all the gruesome details. The sessions were beneficial and there were several things that deeply resonated with me. I can't forget when my therapist said to me that I should ask God what He wants me to do with a story such as mine. I never imagined that I would ever share the details of my story, much less write a whole book. A critical moment of being liberated from the trauma of my past was an activity done during therapy. The conversations about the issue were valuable, but an assignment given from a session was instrumental in kickstarting this book. The assignment was to make a list of all that Keith had done to me. I was reluctant and even felt ashamed to write these things down. They were just too embarrassing and degrading. Nevertheless, I mustered up the courage and began to make that list. With honesty, I dug deep down to excavate my truth and faced it on paper. I desperately wanted to get the story and pain out so badly that I was blatantly honest. I was honest with every bit of it because my intention was to destroy the list afterwards. In my mind, I figured no one would ever read this list. I had to grieve the love I gave Keith over the years we were together. Once the list was done, I felt such a release as I shared it with my therapist. From my experience, healing is more than going to therapy. Healing commenced when I did what was required to rebuild and feel empowered again. Therapy gave me the opportunity to start again, using what was shattered to rebuild a more fortified me.

The inception of this book was disguised as an assignment from the therapy session. This book has given me a canvas to share my story, a story that gave me freedom and an outlet to release all I had inside. I never imagined that writing this book would be the ultimate tool that helped me to overcome depression. Page by page I started to expose the personal wounds, pitfalls, and silent traumas that I have sustained. This tool, my book, provided an avenue for me to release my pain and captured the journey of being restored to an improved version of myself. The scenes of my past no longer looped in my mind. I can truly say it is finished. Finally, I have leaped over the hurdle in releasing my story. After all, behind every dark cloud there is a silver lining. I realized that my book was my silver lining because it gave me a voice. Subsequently, it became a voice to the prospective readers who would now have a point of reference for their own stories. I began to envision how prospective readers would begin to see that possibilities to overcome periods of turbulence do exist. I wanted my readers to know that healing is possible and living after pain is also possible; moreover, that God giving beauty for ashes is possible.

Furthermore, I hope my readers will know that greatness is possible regardless of race, ethnicity, or geographic location and that the possibilities are endless. In the words of Marcus Mosiah Garvey, "Great principles, great ideals know no nationality." It does not matter who you are or where you are from; greatness is possible. I wrote this book with the intention of helping to heal others and give awareness to circumstances like mine. I saw my book as a tool to inspire readers that there is another way of dealing with the lows of life and that there is no need to suffer in silence. Through this book I have gained the insight that no one should be silenced or crippled by the traumas of life but should strive to regain their confidence, restore their hope, and rebuild themselves holistically to live again. With immense passion I wanted to tell readers that seasons of turbulence are like the autumn season, where only the leaves fall off but the whole plant does not die. The tree awaits a shift in the season for spring to emerge with the sprouting of new green leaves and brightly colored petals. The plant lives and blooms again and so can you.

I was fueled with power and confidence as I shared my experience. At last, I owned my story and found purpose and value in my journey. Being empowered, I refused to make my experience become an untold story. The polarity of writing this book made me feel like a part of me died and another part was rebirthed. There was closure in finally putting my past to rest, which laid the foundation for the new and improved version of myself to emerge. Recording my story made me feel like a preserved historic monument. The history of the monument (my story) makes it special but the fact that I still stand today is even more remarkable. Therapy is a time to rebuild; it is a time to start again. It was the time that I started rebuilding my self-esteem, confidence and revamped my personal philosophies. The aftermath of my poor decisions and life experiences left me in ruins, so it was time to rebuild. My bricks were not new; they were broken. Nevertheless, I rebuilt with the broken bricks I had in my hands. Nehemiah used tattered bricks to rebuild the walls of Jerusalem which further inspired me that broken bricks still build.

"Will they revive the stones out of the heaps of rubbish which are burned?"

Nehemiah 4:2 (KJV)

We are still able to rebuild even though our bricks are burnt and tattered. Building with tattered bricks is what makes the monument remarkable. Rebuilding through therapy requires work, much like Nehemiah, who rebuilt the city of Jerusalem. For the city of Jerusalem to be restored, Nehemiah and the Jews had to be relentless to achieve this. Likewise, our restoration requires the work to build again, brick by brick.

Then I said to them, You see the bad situation we are in—how Jerusalem lies in ruins, and its gates are burned with fire. Come, let us build up the wall of Jerusalem, that we may no longer be a disgrace.

Then I told them of the hand of my God which was upon me for good, and also the words that the king had spoken to me. And they said, Let us rise up and build! So they strengthened their hands for the good work.

Nehemiah 2:17-18 (NIV)

It was a struggle to work on the biggest project of my life: this book. I questioned what to write and how to write it. Once I got started, I could not stop. There were times I had a burst of writing sessions and then there were days, and even weeks, I did not write a single word. I encountered silent wrestles of doubts and uncertainty, of whether this book would be read. It took courage to write this book and having courage is challenging. My mind was constantly bombarded with questions like, who will publish my book? Who will read my book? Will my book come to fruition? How would I fund the process? Who will resonate with my story? Why are you working so hard on something where the outcome is unknown? Will it get lost in the abyss of book publications? Though there were many wavering thoughts surrounding this book, I had this unrelenting nudge that would not allow me to give up on it. I have had many pauses, but I always knew I had to finish what I started. I knew that completing this book and getting it published would have been my greatest accomplishment at this point in my life.

Writing this book was like running a marathon, which required the endurance and determination to never stop until I had crossed the finish line. Regardless of the conflicting thoughts, I had to complete the task at hand. I felt like I would have betrayed myself if I had not seen it through to the end. Whenever imposter syndrome stepped in, I wrote like I was not writing about myself. Instead, I wrote from the lens as a bystander who was observing the events of my own life. The courage to continue writing was fueled by just a little hope that there was someone who would be impacted by my story. So, I continued to write regardless of my doubt. I wrote even though I did not know the outcome. I wrote because at night I could not sleep due to the incessant nudges to get my story out. I wrote even though I had no guarantee of the result. Now, this is faith—no guarantee but moving forward anyway. During this time, faith was challenging, because I kept writing even though I did not have all the answers.

Broken Bricks Still Build

Writing this book made me believe in myself. I had countless mental fights with the ideas that this won't sell, or nobody will read it, or there are already enough books out there. My apprehensions were intercepted by a subtle thought saying, look at creation. There are so many trees of the same kind across the globe, but they are all still standing on purpose. Do these trees compete? They do not compete even though they bear the same fruit. The unique thing is that though they bear the same fruit they are serving people for the same reason but in a different location. Right at that moment, I realized that my book would be serving people for a similar reason as other books, but there is an audience to which this book is called. I have come to realize that we do not need to compete and compare, for we all have a unique purpose to fulfill. I really had to double down and believe in myself, which meant reflecting on previous victories. I thought to myself, there were hundreds of classmates when I matriculated into college and upon graduation, I was among the graduates given a bachelor's degree with honors. So, I said to myself, there is greatness in me since I was able to shine with the other graduating stars. In addition to that, I was awarded a full tuition scholarship for three of the four years of my college tenure. Again, I was shining with the other stars in my cohort who acquired said award. I started to reflect more on all that I had achieved thus far. I thought of all the teachers in the world, and there are close to 85 million. I am among the 85 million who are blazing a trail of excellence. So, if there are 85 million teachers and I am one of them, why can't I publish a book and be among the millions of publications? Why not?

I went so far as to think of myself as a driver. At the end of my first week on the road, I thought I would not follow through with driving. Nevertheless, I did not quit and kept driving just about every day. Now today I am still driving among the estimated 1.4 billion drivers in the world. So, my question again? Why can't I publish this book and have it be among the millions of books published? It is safe to say that my reflection on past challenges conquered contributed to the confidence that pushed me to continue writing this book and make it become a reality. The moral of the story is that the firmament spreads wide, and there is a place for all stars to shine. There is no need to be intimidated by all other stars because we are all shining stars. Even though the stars are vast and numerous, God knows every single one by name. (Psalm 147:4 NKJV) He counts the number of the stars; He calls them all by name. There are approximately 200 billion trillion stars in the universe; all have a place and are shining with splendor. So, what about you and me, who God also knows by name? Our names are written on the palms of His hands.

> *"See, I have written your name on the palms of my hands. Always in my mind is a picture of Jerusalem's walls in ruins."*
>
> Isaiah 49:16 (NLT)

God makes the 200 billion trillion stars shine; what more will He do with just eight billion people? The stars in the firmament teach us a lesson: that we must overcome intimidating thoughts because all stars shine with splendor. The Earth and all creation eagerly await the manifestation of the sons of God. (Romans 8:19 NLT) For all creation is waiting eagerly for that future day when God will reveal who His children really are. We often don't recognize how awesome we are, just as how the butterfly doesn't see the beauty in its wings. So, here is a shout out to all the stars; let's take our place and shine. Believe in yourself!

> *"Butterflies can't see their wings. They can't see how truly beautiful they are, but everyone else can. People are like that as well."*
>
> —Naya Rivera

Another major thing from therapy that helped me in overcoming depression was a session where I uncovered my interests and leisure activities. As I rediscovered myself, I learned to take inventory of my own abilities and capabilities. I started working towards maximizing my talents and the opportunities at my fingertips. I had the intentional mindset to work on what I already had and to continue the quest of discovering my hidden abilities. A pivotal conversation in the session surrounded my love for playing the piano. She asked how I learned to play, and I told her my dad taught me. She encouraged me to start playing the piano again at least a couple times per week, as well as to consider playing for an audience.

After my parents' separation and subsequent divorce, I felt like I had lost my daddy. Thereafter, the relationship between my dad and me gradually eroded. It was like a ship that had drifted far away from the docks. A little girl who once jumped on her daddy's back laughing from ear to ear, who cried to say "see you later" when dropped off at school, had now lost her dad. The little girl who anxiously checked the refrigerator for a treat Daddy brought in after late hours at work was missing her dad. Her superhero seemed to have taken flight, even though in plain sight, because I was living with a void inside; a void that lasted fourteen years surely created anger, bitterness, and hurt. I never imagined that a gap so extensive would ever converge. During therapy my therapist inquired about the relationship with my father. She asked why I did not reach out for his help during the relationship with Keith. I explained to her that there was a breakdown in our relationship that hindered this type of communication. This was a prompt to reflect on the relationship with my father. Consequently, I made the conscious decision to focus on how Daddy had positively impacted my life throughout the years.

The irony is that now that I had moved over a thousand miles away from my family, I finally felt like I got my dad back. One could ask how that is possible. The isolation from everything I knew, family, friends and my home country, required me to make a quick yet grounded decision to sink or swim. As I tried to kickstart and navigate this new transition, my choices were tied to how Daddy navigated life. I remembered the wisdom from his past life experiences on how he overcame the challenges of his childhood and even in his adult life. My father left his blueprint in my heart based on how I saw him navigating life, a blueprint that can never be erased. The lessons he taught stuck with me, and the wisdom of his experiences guided me in making important decisions. Whenever I needed to make a decision, I asked myself what Daddy would do in this situation. Each time, it felt like he was right there as my coach, to provide guidance or question a decision I was about to make. Daddy's blueprint was very evident in my choices.

The relationship between my dad and me started to heal while I was over a thousand miles away. Our father-daughter piano lessons were revamped, partially inspired by encouragement from my therapist. My father and I were virtually meeting every Sunday at 4 p.m. sharp for my piano lessons. He was always a man of time who did not like being late for anything. My online piano lessons were for one hour where I gleaned musical knowledge from my dad the expert pianist. Our sessions were filled with laughter as my dad became my musical mentor. Growing up, I always admired my father's playing, which motivated me to mimic his style. One of my favorite memories of playing the piano as a child was when there was a lesson that required the instructor (my dad) to accompany the student (me). Those were my favorite lessons because once my dad started to accompany the musical piece, it sounded so rich with all the advanced chords the instructor (my dad) added. I would bubble inside and overflow with joy as we played these melodies, harmonizing bar by bar. Since I admired my dad's playing style so much, I often stretched for his advanced piano books. I remember his piano books entitled *Greatest Songs of All Times* and *Greatest RnB Hits*. Of course, these songs were too advanced for me to play, but I would sit at the piano as I tried to decipher the chords or read the musical score. Sometimes I got overwhelmed and took a break for a while, but I would always try again another day.

When I was growing up my dad also worked as a cocktail pianist. There were nights when he could not find his music books for his performances. His books were missing. Missing? Yes. Earlier that day I would have taken the books from his trunk and tried to play these hit songs. Innocently, I forgot to return his books as they were left on the piano in the house. These piano lessons between my dad and me played an important part in my healing journey. Finally, I got my dad back and I felt equipped to play the piano again. I started learning new songs on the piano, embellished with the chords my dad taught me. This hobby contributed to personal fulfillment and pushed me a step further in becoming self-actualized. Moreover, playing the piano again helped to keep my mental health in check.

Since ancient times music has been found to have therapeutic benefits. Studies have shown that Greek physicians have used several musical instruments to heal their patients. Furthermore, Aristotle postulated in one of his books that music can quicken emotions and purify the soul. Playing the piano again was a soothing experience, as I listened to and enjoyed my own playing. Am I the best pianist? Absolutely not. One thing, though, I will never stop playing. Ultimately, when I reflect on the contributions my dad has made to my life, he has shaped me in countless ways. I choose to focus on the positives; the good times Daddy and I had. I will always reflect on the fun memories of Daddy teaching me to swim, ride a bike, and navigate life. The truth is Daddy taught me well and celebrated even small wins. For instance, after we got back from a driving lesson one day, Daddy made a "huge" announcement to everyone. He exclaimed, "Guess what happened this morning? Shawna overtook an eighteen-wheeler on the highway!" Of course, we all burst out laughing, because Daddy always finds a comical way to express celebrations.

As I continued learning to maneuver driving, there were moments when Daddy had to quickly intervene because I was headed into oncoming traffic. Thank God Daddy was able to step in, in the nick of time. As my driving skills became sharper, I glimpsed out the corner of my eyes and saw Daddy's hand hovering over the emergency brake. I felt reassured knowing that Daddy was there to correct potential mistakes. These are the memories I'm choosing to cherish; these are the moments that warm my heart. As I continue this path of healing, I am making the deliberate choice to focus on the positives. Adopting the honeybee mindset in contrast to the fruit fly's mindset paved the way for the change in our father-daughter relationship.

In an environment filled with debris, the honeybee will seek out the nectar of flowers. Comparatively, regardless of the friction in the relationship with my father, I chose to focus on the positives of our relationship. In making this decision, our relationship has transformed over the years, and I can truly say that Daddy is not just my father but also my bona fide friend. Conversely, the fruit fly mindset would have perpetuated the discord in our father-daughter relationship. Since the fruit fly seeks out the garbage and passes over the nectar of the flower, this mindset would be the recipe to stay in depression. Focusing on the positives overrides the negative, which provides an improved outlook on challenging circumstances.

In Philippians 4 we are encouraged to think on things that are honorable, right, pure, lovely, and admirable. Fixing my eyes on these things freed me from offense in my heart that only cost me the wellbeing of my mind.

"And now, dear brothers and sisters, one final thing. Fix your thoughts on what is true, and honorable, and right, and pure, and lovely, and admirable. Think about things that are excellent and worthy of praise."

Philippians 4:8 (NLT)

BROKEN BRICKS STILL BUILD

The taunting memories from the relationship with Keith were further extinguished by a message preached by Bishop T.D Jakes in 1996. It was 2021 when I was watching this sermon. It is undeniable that it was the power of the Holy Spirit that led me to this message. The whole sermon was impactful, but the zenith was the deliverance at the end. T.D Jakes made an altar call to release persons suffering from memories of their pasts. I burst into tears. I cried, and then I cried some more. I knew this was divine. I felt as though I was at this altar call with everyone else. The message was preached 25 years prior, and it was as if God had this lined up for my deliverance in 2021.

As time progressed, I continued to process the pain of my relationship with Keith. There was another encounter that I believed helped to sever me from the taunting memories of Keith. On several occasions I had dreams where Keith was harming me in some way. However, I had a particular dream where Keith was about to attack me. He called out some other men to help him. I started to yell "Call the police! Call the police!" When I looked around, I saw an army of uniformed soldiers marching armed with their guns. One of the soldiers shot Keith right away and he instantly fell, wabbling on the ground. The other men with Keith dropped their weapons immediately with expressions of surrender. I cannot resist believing that this dream had a real connection in setting me free from the literal nightmares of Keith.

One of the biggest turning points in overcoming depression was finding purpose. I started to realize that I was created intentionally with a purpose. At times I became distracted by looking at what was going on in everyone else's life. My thoughts were redirected when the conscious decision was made to unlock and walk in the path God designed for me. I refused to allow my destiny to be left locked up and not serving its intended purpose. The shark rules the sea, the eagle rules the air, the lion rules the jungle. All are top predators that have a unique niche in the ecosystem. Each of these predators dominate in their distinctive environments. If any of these three were to be completely displaced in trying to fit the mold of the other, the whole ecosystem would collapse.

This analogy is comparable to the unique purpose in each of our lives. We all need to tap into that unique purpose according to the plan that God has for us. I found purpose in my story, and I diligently worked to see its fruition. I believed there was purpose in my story, and I acted on said belief. Walking in purpose is walking in faith. It is God that orchestrates our destiny, but we must act by faith for its manifestation. The steps we take by faith towards our destiny breathe life into the plan God has for us. Believing without action is futile.

> *"What good is it, dear brothers and sisters, if you say you have faith but don't show it by your actions? Can that kind of faith save anyone?"*
>
> James 2:14 (NLT)

Recognizing the value in my story gave me permission to share my story. Though pain was intertwined in my story, God had a plan to birth purpose through its sting. I finally found the courage, boldness, and confidence to share what I so desperately wanted to discard and keep hidden. Undoubtedly, sharing my story was for my healing; moreover, it was for the audience who will resonate with the intricacies of it all.

> *"For I know the plans I have for you'" says the Lord. 'They are plans for good and not for disaster, to give you a future and a hope.'"*
>
> Jeremiah 29:11 (NLT)

Bishop RC Blakes Jr. speaks and writes passionately to encourage women to have a queen-conscious mindset. He was a dominant voice that helped me regained my confidence as a single woman. (In chapter 11 I will expound more on navigating life as a single woman.) His conversations surround self-love, regaining confidence, healing from trauma, and becoming a virtuous woman. Through his messages, I recognized my value and was empowered to not shortchange myself by making poor relational choices. I became dedicated to investing in myself, because I had grown to love me. I loved who I saw in the mirror; moreover I loved the woman I was becoming as my self-confidence improved.

In becoming this confident woman, there were persons who did not understand or support my journey. This meant moving on with questions unanswered, without explanations or even apologies from these individuals. For once, I was living life on my terms without allowing the perspectives of others to hinder my evolution. I started to live life with intentionality and being okay to disappoint others. This meant saying no and taking a confident stance on things important to me. If I was consumed with appeasing everyone, I would have disappointed myself. Acquiescing to how others think I should live life would have prevented me from being true to who I am at the core. I continued to invest in myself through books and listening to different impactful speakers. The wisdom gleaned positively influenced my self-confidence and changed my distorted ideologies. There were no short cuts to gaining self-confidence. It was achieved over time through gaining insight that could be applied to my life. Getting to the other side of self-confidence meant making new choices and being enthusiastic about the results of those choices.

As my self-confidence grew, I became more selective about the voices that had access to me. I sought wise counsel to further contribute to a positive mindset. This meant avoiding conversations of pessimism or destructive criticism. Maintaining this choice came with resistance, but my response was to be resolute in my decision. These choices set the stage for me to attain personal goals and become assertive in who I was becoming. It was necessary for improving my mental health and establishing boundaries for my own self-preservation.

Making the wise choice of choosing all that adds value to us plays an integral role in building self-confidence. Being involved in communities where there is an exchange of wisdom and positivity is imperative in building and sustaining confidence. Proverbs 27 speaks to the benefits of surrounding ourselves with individuals who are positive; inspiring circles promote confidence.

"As iron sharpens iron, so a friend sharpens a friend."

Proverbs 27:17 (NLT)

Books, motivational speeches, podcasts, and communities will absolutely inspire, empower, and motivate. Ultimately, only God takes us through the journey of solidifying our healing. God is an integral part of my journey in rebuilding from the broken experiences of life. Intentionally, I immersed myself in scriptures, where my mind was renewed. This helped with my identity, self- image, self-worth, and vision for my life. Specifically, I found identity as a virtuous woman through the lens of the Proverbs 31 woman. I recognized the parallel in the character and integrity I possessed with that of this virtuous woman. The Proverbs 31 woman is often used as the standard for women to esteem themselves in preparation for marriage. However, I had been transformed to reflect the qualities of this virtuous woman outside the context of marriage. I identify with this woman of dignity, work ethic, and noble character.

As I matured into being a virtuous woman, I was able to forgive myself for my poor decisions of the past. I saw the grace that covered my mistakes and decided to continue walking in it. This set me free from self-pity and destructive self-talk. I love and appreciate myself because finally, I recognized God's love for me and took it personally. Through God's Word, I felt seen and chosen when I witnessed how God refashioned me into a virtuous woman. In hindsight, it was obvious that my choices earlier in life were without Godly wisdom; however, today I stand as a transformed version of myself—a virtuous woman.

As a new version of myself, I am better equipped at navigating life God's way. With this renewed mindset, I am continually being affirmed through the promises and assurance found in scriptures. I will be forever reassured that regardless of future broken experiences, God will always heal our broken hearts and stitch up our wounds (Psalm 147: 3). Allowing God's Word to heal our hearts is possible, because there were times when all I knew were sorrows. I went through a period when I lost my smile and was sad most of the time. Everything started to change once I believed that I would see the goodness of the Lord in the land of the living (Psalm 27:13). This gave me the hope that better days were indeed ahead. I was empowered to endure the healing journey and trusted that my today would not be my tomorrow.

For so many years, I desperately wanted to forget the harrowing romance of my past. I questioned myself repeatedly, why can't I just forget the pain and the trauma? The solution to this lingering pain was knowing that though I have miseries, in Christ I will only remember them as water that passed by (Job 11:16). Without this knowledge in Christ, I would not have received the comfort I so desperately yearned for.

"Because you would forget your misery and remember it as waters that have passed away."

Job 11:16 (NKJV)

This scripture was the weapon that defended my mind from the debilitating memories of my past romance. This text provided the liberation needed to see my misery as waters that had passed away. These memories were not forgotten, but were neutralized when God's truth was internalized in my heart. God changed the narrative when He transformed my painful memories into this book. It was after this project that I could really see my misery as water that had passed away.

It is certain that God transforms the pain of our brokenness into purpose. Nevertheless, He requires us to assemble those broken bricks so He can change the narrative of our stories. Finding purpose from the tumultuous relationship with Keith is the epitome of extracting beauty from ashes. Therapy helped me perceive the beauty camouflaged in the ashes of my trauma. I assembled my broken bricks in writing and sharing my story for the first time. We overcome by the blood of the Lamb and the word of our testimony (Revelation 12:11).

How will you reassemble your broken bricks?

Broken Bricks Still Build!

Chapter 9

———∽∞∾———

Coming to America

Great is Thy faithfulness, O God my Father;
there is no shadow of turning with Thee;
Thou changest not, Thy compassions, they fail not;
as Thou hast been, Thou forever wilt be.

Thomas O. Chisholm

New beginnings are often marked with the opportunity for a fresh start. Migrating to America was a new beginning with much excitement and suspense. In August 2019, I took the risk and challenge of moving to a new country alone. It was only a few months prior that I deferred acceptance to a master's program to further my studies in education. I made the choice to accept employment in the United States. This relocation was due to a career opportunity in education. At that time, it had been nine years since I took the detour of enrolling into a bachelor of education program. Here I was nine years later in route to North Carolina. Thanks to a teaching program sponsor, I was afforded a one-way ticket connecting in Fort Lauderdale and then to North Carolina. Having a bachelor's degree in education was an imperative prerequisite for applying and being accepted into a teaching program in the United States. Throughout my teaching career, I frequently heard of international teaching programs. However, this venture was not my aspiration, therefore I did not initiate an application. Even during my tenure at college, I recall one of our lecturers saying "Some of you will teach abroad in the United States." I did not give much thought to this statement, because I never expected to be an international educator. My unsuspecting mind could not recognize that a seed was planted to be realized nine years later.

During the first year of my teaching career, the opportunity of teaching abroad came across my path. Once again, I disregarded the thought. Firstly, I felt scared, intimated, and inadequate to launch out to teach in the great U.S.A. Secondly, I was ineligible to apply because at that time I was an inexperienced educator, had insufficient funds, and was not a licensed driver. These hindrances made me acquiesce into thinking I would not be an ideal candidate as an international educator. Several years passed, and the thoughts of becoming an international educator faded away. One night, as I stood by my kitchen window and gazed into the dark skies, something said to me, your degree is a ticket. I said to myself, a ticket??? The more I thought of it, the more it seemed to be possible. It was a light bulb moment when I recognized the possibility of this becoming a reality.

Sometime later, a colleague persistently urged me to submit an application to become an international educator. On multiple occasions she would see me and say, "You need to apply to the program!" She added, "You look like someone who should apply." Every time we encountered each other she greeted me with the encouragement to put in an application. This colleague seemed like she was mandated to ensure that I applied. One night as I lay in bed, I was scrolling on Facebook. There was an advertisement for a company that sponsored international teachers for the United States. I nonchalantly filled out the application form and hit the submit button. There was no response for a few months and once again I thought it was not going to happen.

Eventually I got a response from the sponsor and started the process of submitting the required documents. As the process progressed, several interviews were undertaken, and I landed a teaching position in North Carolina. Now, this is what you call stumbling upon an opportunity. There was no foreknowledge of this company; I just stumbled into them. I literally scrolled my way into this opportunity. It would seem to be serendipitous, but in hindsight it was the providence of God carefully ordering my steps. Becoming an international educator became a reality through an orchestrated scroll on Facebook. I never thought being an international educator would be a part of my story. Even in my penultimate and ultimate year of the teaching program it still felt unreal. I just never had the wildest dream or even considered that I would live in the United States.

As preparations were made to transition from Jamaica to the United States, my father ensured everything was copacetic for my departure. He was the contact person for selling my car and ensured I was not being ripped off. Subsequently, he became my driver after the sale. From the start, Daddy supported me with words of encouragement and affirmation until the day he dropped me off at the airport. In this chapter I will share my journey of coming to America and my experience while living there.

During the 21 days of fasting at our church in January 2019, there was a session with our bishop and pastor. One of our tasks was to write down what we were fasting for. I recorded that I needed a sense of direction and guidance for my life and career path. When there were three days remaining in the fast, I received an email from the sponsor for international teachers. This email initiated the process of submitting required documents for migrating to the United States. It was the start of the transition of my life and career according to my request at the beginning of the fast.

As preparations were under way, it was time to consider the sale of my car. Interestingly, the sale of the car was finalized before my interview at the U.S. embassy. It was a challenging move of faith. It was a faith move for two reasons. Selling the car meant I was moving forward and believing that the Lord was ordering my steps into this new transition. Secondly, there was a document required by the embassy from the sponsor for the interview. However, there was a delay in the delivery of this document. I was a bit on edge, because my preference was to receive this document prior to selling the car. At the same time, there was another thought saying the document would not arrive until the car was sold. I believe that my threshold of faith was being stretched. A buyer was sent, and the car was sold before I received the document in hand. Now I had the check for the sale, yet I was so concerned about not receiving that document. Here is proof that my faith was being stretched. Later in the afternoon on the same day that the car was sold, I got an email from the sponsor. I was informed that the document was sent off and should be in my possession within a few days.

It was departure day and I hustled through the airport with my two suitcases. Through the window of the aircraft, I admired the picturesque view of my home country while taking off into the unknown. I was nervous and anxious about what lay ahead at the destination in North Carolina. This was my second time traveling outside of Jamaica, and the uncertainties made me apprehensive. Coincidentally, I bumped into two Jamaican guys at the Fort Lauderdale airport. One of the guys inquired if I was a participant on the teaching program. Simultaneously, they both confirmed to be participants as well. I was relieved. At last, I had travel companions to allay my anxieties who were more experienced travelers than I was. So, we hung out together at the airport in Fort Lauderdale, getting food and chit chatting as we awaited our next flight to North Carolina. As we waited at the gate for our next flight, I got in touch with my family to keep them up to date with the progress on my travel. Thank God these two guys were experienced travelers, because they realized that the gate for our flight had changed online. We all rushed to the new gate just in time to be in the last batch of passengers to board the flight. I got to my seat, but to my surprise there was another passenger already seated in my seat. We checked our boarding passes and realized that both passengers were assigned the same seat. The flight attendant rectified the matter, and I was assigned to another seat.

Was this it? No. At my new seat I tried to fit my carry on into the overhead cabin. I struggled until I eventually beckoned the flight attendant again for assistance. My carry on ended up being tucked somewhere around the back. With a sigh of relief, I sat and was ready to go. By this time, I was tired and just could not wait to arrive at the destination.

As the aircraft prepared to land in Raleigh, North Carolina I looked out the windows and could see the layout of the city. My imagination kept creating images of the unseen and the unknown. Upon landing in Raleigh, I saw a few familiar faces of other teachers I knew as we claimed our luggage. My anxiety was still high, and I wondered what I had gotten myself into. I eventually saw the ambassadors for the program dressed in their sponsor shirts and badges, who I recognized from previous video calls. By this time, I had collected all my luggage and awaited directives. As the international teachers boarded the bus to be transported to the hotel for accommodation, I was still anxious. We finally arrived at the hotel where we were greeted by the CEO and other members of the sponsoring company. I collected other important documents and was handed my room key. I got to my room, took a deep breath, and realized I had finally made it.

That night I fell to my knees and gave God thanks for His journeying mercies and protection for taking me this far. Afterwards, I refreshed myself and went back to the lobby area to chit chat with the other international educators. That night I had my first chicken sandwich at the famous Chick-fil-A. The cohort of international teachers were engaged in orientation sessions with the program sponsor for a few days. Thereafter, we headed off to our individual counties to embark on the new experience of being international educators.

Being a new international teacher to the county, attendance at additional orientation was necessary for sensitization to policies and expectations. From the very first day of school, everything was fast paced, and there was a lot to learn. I found myself power walking down the hallways to get tasks done faster. I had new colleagues to meet, lesson plans to be made, meetings to attend, mandatory professional development courses to complete, and new students to face. Immediately, I noticed the huge culture gap. For me to be an efficient and impactful educator, I had to revolutionize my teaching methodologies, attune myself to the new curriculum, and learn to tackle the antics of middle school children.

Building the student-teacher relationship was the hard part. Generation Z are not very motivated in getting formal education, plus here comes their new teacher with a Caribbean accent. Therefore, I had to communicate succinctly, being intentional with my diction and enunciation. It was imperative to find creative ways of incorporating aspects of my Jamaican culture in the classroom as well as answering their inquisitive questions.

Interestingly, as time elapsed, I became the mediator and mentor in my classroom, especially when cultural differences arose among our mixed group of students. I also believe that my presence in the classroom motivated some students to strive for excellence and overcome any limitations that may hinder their path to success. Sharing aspects of my Jamaican culture on countless occasions have broadened the horizons of their thinking. During these conversations, nuggets of wisdom that are applicable in their lives were transferred to students. Throughout the years of being an international educator, I believe that I have inspired students and staff to be attuned to some qualities of being global citizens in our world today. Overcoming the steep learning curve of the culture and instructional practices while getting my personal affairs in order was not easy. I had become so acclimatized to being on the go that one morning I jumped out of bed and hustled to get ready for the day. To my surprise it was Saturday morning.

There was a stark difference between Raleigh and the county where I was assigned to teach. My assignment was in a very rural county. This place was uncomfortable, inconvenient, and the way of life was nothing like I expected. I felt awkward and out of place, as though I was dropped off in the middle of nowhere. There was nothing in sight that resembled back home. I could not believe there was no public transportation—no buses, taxis, nor Uber. I did not know how to find my way around and I did not have a car.

My next mission was to get my North Carolina driver's license. I rented a car for a week and depended solely on the GPS navigation. In learning to get around, I was frequently lost and became frustrated. Furthermore, I had to constantly remind myself to stay on the ride side of the road since we drive on the left side in Jamaica. Being lost in a new country made me feel even more isolated. I had the afterthought of using the rental car for my driving test later that week. By the time I had this thought I only had two days left with the rental car. Additionally, I was not entirely prepared for the written part of the driving test. So, I did my best to go through the driver's handbook and watched YouTube videos.

These few days of preparation meant I had to be laser focused on this test. I had to double down and do what the present moment required of me. Not knowing anything about cars, it was my father who guided me in purchasing my car after I got my license. Instead of the city life I anticipated, I was placed in an agricultural community where the locals raised cows, pigs, chickens, and used pick-up trucks to transport hay. Daytime and night were quiet; however, sunrise and sunset were marked by the crowing of my neighbor's rooster. Additionally, as I drove to and from work there were acres of farmland on both sides, with cows grazing on grass; on several occasions, there were eighteen wheelers transporting pigs pulling onto the highway. One of the first things that teachers and parents asked was, "How did you get all the way out here?" They would follow up with the statement, "You must be a brave young lady to be out here by yourself."

Having made the move to the United States, I was living on my own without friends and family. Being in a country that is so unfamiliar, it was difficult to adjust to the culture, climate, and to simple day-to-day living. I became homesick, and my taste buds longed for my favorite Jamaican snacks. With online shopping, sometimes it took up to six weeks for them to arrive; nevertheless, when they did I felt a little closer to home. I missed home, the food, the laughter of the people, the warmth, and our beautiful sunshine. Not seeing or hearing anything that reminded me of home made me feel isolated and even lost at times. With social media, I got a taste of home through hearing authentic Jamaican jokes and just being kept in the loop of current affairs. I also got the opportunity of joining fellow countrymen of the Jamaican diaspora to virtually experience parts of our culture. This made me feel at home at last.

Adjusting to the climate was particularly difficult, because as an island girl I was not accustomed to the low temperatures. So, my new style included getting dressed in layers of clothes and I had to make sure the car engine was warmed up during winter. The winter of 2022 was the worst. It was the coldest temperature I had ever experienced, due to a devastating winter storm that holiday weekend. The mayor of Buffalo, New York described it as the blizzard of the century. With temperatures between 12-14^{0}F, I tried to stay warm as I recovered from pneumonia. My heating unit blew cold air and eventually the power went out for about four hours. That winter season caught me off guard, but I survived as the storm blew over and I gradually regained my health.

It was not long before I could feel rejection from some students and staff. The condescending looks and tones showed that my presence was not approved. I felt as though I was invited but not welcomed in this working environment. Common courtesy in the workplace was quite nominal. I was not just a black woman, but a black woman who came from a small Caribbean Island, a third world country. I remember a coworker saying to me face to face, "Isn't Jamaica just a dot on the map?" Which was followed by her gestures of making a staccato dot in air with her finger. She added, "Aren't you guys scared that the island will sink?"

I am not sure of her motive in saying these words to me. But what I know for sure is that my humble beginnings have taught me life lessons that will forever be engraved in my heart. Coming from humble beginnings gave me the determination, fight and grit I have today. My years spent in Jamaica undoubtably prepared me for surviving and thriving in the bigger world that I now found myself. I was now able to extrapolate the wisdom from my life in Jamaica to my new reality of living in the U.S. Life in Jamaica equipped me with wittiness of mind, innovation, and quick thinking, which I for sure needed at this time. I also remember a teacher saying to me "You are smart." Her expressions showed surprise and disbelief.

In Jamaica we often say *don't watch the noise of the market, watch your profit.* This was reflected at the end of the academic year 2020-2021 in the Covid-19 pandemic. That year I was the only teacher in the school building who demonstrated progress in student test scores. It was my first end of grade test, since testing in 2019-2020 was cancelled due to the pandemic. Furthermore, in my final year of the teaching program, my principal informed me that my students had the highest growth in the end of grade science test in the entire county. In the words of Marcus Mosiah Garvey, "*Great principles, great ideals know no nationality.*" It does not matter your nationality; greatness is possible. Throughout the tenure of this teaching program, I was bombarded with so many inappropriate questions and remarks from students and staff. Do you have clean drinking water in Jamaica? Do you wear shoes in Jamaica? Do you have roads in Jamaica? Why did you come here? How many universities are in Jamaica? And the questions went on. A student went as far as telling me that I needed to straighten my hair. There were so many mornings I cried on my way to work and then dried my tears before getting out of the car. In tears, I wondered what I had gotten myself into. I questioned if I had made the right decision in coming to America. I even felt scrutinized in the church community. One Sunday as I walked in a service, members of the congregation looked at me as though I had lost my way and stumbled into the church. When I looked around, I was the only black person in the church. On many occasions I felt ostracized because of my accent, nationality, and the melanin in my skin. All this ranged from the mocking remarks from the students, inappropriate questions and comments from staff, everyday interactions when conducting business and being observed like a specimen at a science exposition.

At the start of the teaching program, three Jamaican teachers, including myself, were assigned to the same school. By the time five years had elapsed, I was the only one left. The other two had discontinued their participation in the program. I did not stay because I was treated well or embraced. I stayed because I was on assignment. Underneath the hostility, I was developing roots for endurance and perseverance. Enduring these pressures served as the substratum for my character development, patience, compassion, and self-confidence through Christ. I learned to focus on my audience of One (Jesus Christ) until I became resistant against the negativity. Was I tempted to resign? Absolutely! In fact, I made several attempts to reach out to other schools for a transfer. However, there was always a subtle urge that said I must see this season through to the end. So, I remained planted, at this school and in the Word of God. I developed a refuse to lose mindset, where I did what was needed of me to endure until the end. Ecclesiastes 7:8 speaks about the end of a thing being better than the start of that thing. This kept me motivated to be committed to complete this season of my life and not to exit prematurely. I constantly reminded myself that I must complete what I started.

"Better is the end of a thing than the beginning thereof: and the patient in spirit is better than the proud in spirit."

Ecclesiastes 7:8 (KJV)

Being committed to this five-year isolation reminded me of the fall of Jericho. In Joshua 6, the Lord told Joshua that the Israelites would have victory over Jericho. However, it required their commitment to march around the city once per day for six days and then seven times on the seventh day. The Israelites had to remain committed during every lap. They could not stop in the fifth lap and say they had marched enough and demand victory. They had to remain committed until every single lap was completed and they had followed all the other requirements. How do we know they were committed? According to the scriptures, they were faithful in completing every lap, along with the other instructions, and received the victory that was promised.

Many times, as I endured these five years, I asked God if this was how it's really supposed to be. Am I supposed to feel so isolated and lonely? Should I really remain in a place of rejection and discrimination? Should I remain in the place of being mishandled and misunderstood? Should I remain in a place of being undermined and underestimated? I even had the audacity to ask God if He was sure that I was on the right journey. I know that sounds sacrilegious but frankly speaking, it was so uncomfortable and agonizing. I kept checking in with God to see if this is what He really had in mind all along. The life of Job is quite parallel to this time in my life. Job endured loss after loss and sustained extensive sickness. He suffered for a prolonged period, asked very pressing questions of God, and expressed the distress in his heart.

Job 6:2-3 (NLT) "If my misery could be weighed and my troubles be put on the scales, they would outweigh all the sands of the sea. That is why I spoke impulsively."

Similarly, I questioned God and expressed the sorrows in my heart as I walked through these five years of isolation. Job had motivated me to be faithful during this time and to see it through to the end. As I continued to examine the life of Job, I found the reassurance that God restores. Job's endurance through his season of adversity afforded him the testimony that God knows the path he takes. This inspired my faith where I understood the necessity to trust God's way even in affliction.

"So the Lord blessed Job in the second half of his life even more than in the beginning.

Job lived 140 years after that, living to see four generations of his children and grandchildren. Then he died, an old man who had lived a long, full life."

Job 42:12;16-17 (NLT)

Alternatively, there were times when I really felt my faith slipping away. But Job taught me to keep the faith, to contend for the faith. Even though I did not see the other side, there was a shadow of hope from Job's faithfulness to still believe that God knows the path I take. Coming to America was stepping out on faith like Peter stepped out of the boat and walked on water. To survive this move of faith, I kept my eyes glued to Jesus and though at times I felt my faith slipping, I kept pressing to still believe that God knows the path I take. I kept believing that God did not just bring me this far. I had to keep believing there was something greater on the other side of this submission. Job stayed the course; so, I will stay the course too. It was not so much the lust of the eyes, flesh, and the pride of life that targeted my faith. It was the discomfort in staying the course of submission to this turbulent path God was taking me down. It was relinquishing what I thought this experience would offer. I struggled in the pressing and contemplated giving up and going back home.

In *Acres of Diamonds*, Pastor Jentezen Franklin writes:

If God called you to a certain place, to a certain relationship, to a certain job, to a certain dream, to a certain community, no matter how unfruitful it may look to you on the outside, you stay right where you are. You don't quit. You don't pack your bags. You don't go somewhere else that looks better.

You stay. When everyone else has left, you stay. When you are in a drought and there is no sign of rain, you stay.[4]

Acres of Diamonds provided much of the encouragement that showed me there was purpose in me staying in this county. This book collided with my cry of despair, as I pondered why I should remain there. Reading this book showed me the speck of light at the end of the tunnel. It was during this adversity that I learned to fight with the armor of peace. Instead of retaliating physically to the experience of my environment, I coped by finding solace in the scriptures. In this part of the journey, I recognized that peace is a weapon. It was the weapon that protected me from the unfavorable conditions.

Looking back, the people who rejected me gave me reasons to have offense and bitterness in my heart towards them, but I choose to think of them with compassion instead of anger. I have matured in my faith and have allowed the scriptures to rule in my heart, which governed my actions, thoughts, and words. In Ephesians 6 we are reminded that we are not fighting against flesh and blood but against evil rulers of the unseen world. In this fight peace is listed as a defense.

"Therefore, put on every piece of God's armor so you will be able to resist the enemy in the time of evil... For shoes, put on the peace that comes from the Good News so that you will be fully prepared."

Ephesians 6:13;15 (NLT)

It was only five months after coming to America that the Covid-19 pandemic hit. Living alone through this global catastrophe caused much consternation at the idea of what would happen should I

---

4 Jentezen Franklin, *Acres of Diamonds (2020). 55*

contract Covid-19. My anxiety was exacerbated when colleagues and students became infected. In some cases, even the parents of students passed away. It was also very overwhelming to be barred from family when the borders to Jamaica were closed. Just as I was becoming acclimatized to teaching in the United States, Covid-19 changed everything. The teaching and learning process transitioned to online learning. This shift required me to pivot and readjust teaching methodologies again by utilizing various online learning platforms. Teachers were expected to maintain standards in the execution of online lessons and were held accountable by administrators who would virtually observe sessions.

In addition to delivering the curriculum online, paper packets were prepared and distributed to students without internet access. Teachers were teaching the curriculum by any means necessary. Teachers, including myself, rode the school bus to deliver packets to students in their communities. Upon completion of assignments, the school bus picked up packets which were then dropped off at the school. These packets were placed in a heated room for a determined period. Teachers then collected students' packets and did evaluations for assignments. Time elapsed and the Covid-19 cases plummeted. The second shift occurred when our school transitioned to hybrid learning. During this time teacher-student engagements included both virtual and face-to-face learning. Being back in the school building, members of staff and students wore masks and interactions were uneasy.

The moment that impacted my Christian walk the most was the five years of isolation in North Carolina. It was during this period that I started to evangelize. I evangelized through the *Teach the Nations; Build the Church* podcast. I passed out tracts to my neighbors, co-workers, at the car dealership, at Walmart, and restaurants. I faced sickness, but I also experienced healing. In chapter 10 I will expound more about my healing journey.

I grew deeper in Christ to know Him and developed the sincere desire for others to know Him too. I have no greater desire than to remain and dwell in God's house and to tell others of this Lord and Savior Jesus Christ who saved me and turned my life around. There was a point in this journey that has significantly marked my life forever. I recall one month as I was budgeting and when I got to the end of the spreadsheet the numbers were in the negative. I had never seen this before. I became anxious and said, "That means I will not be able to tithe." In my eyes I just did not have enough. With my finite mind I thought God would allow this thought to just slip by. One day as I was in the restroom at work, I paused and looked in the mirror. For some reason I said, "You know what, I am going to the tithe because in Your Word You said You will provide." I began to remember past testimonies of how God provided for persons who were faced with similar circumstances. So, I boldly said to God, "I am going to tithe and see what You are going to do." I said what I said and left the restroom.

A few weeks after I had that conversation with God several things occurred that confirmed that God is faithful. To start, I was paid for after-school tutoring and in previous years teachers were not paid. Summer school was approaching, where the original plan was for science to be taught for only one week. This meant I would be paid for only one week of summer school. Just as summer school was about to begin, I was informed that a new decision was made, and science would be offered for the duration of summer school. I was paid for over five weeks for summer school. In addition, teachers received two bonuses for the period of summer school they taught. In retrospect, I know without doubt that God had honored my sacrifice and obedience in my tithing.

"Bring all the tithes into the storehouse so there will be enough food in my Temple. If you do,' says the Lord of Heaven's Armies, 'I will open the windows of heaven for

you. I will pour out a blessing so great you won't have enough room to take it in! Try it! Put me to the test!"

Malachi 3:10 (NLT)

As the months progressed in the Covid-19 pandemic my finances were still looking shaky. I did all I could to cut expenses. The last cut I made was disconnecting my internet service and turning in the equipment. One day as I opened the mailbox there was a letter from the internet company. The letter stated the potential of being eligible for $0.00 per month and provided an invitation for me to call. I was not very motivated to call because zero dollars per month just seems too good to be true. It is customary for companies to use these tactics to lure customers into purchasing various internet packages, so I hesitated to make the call. Reluctantly, I decided to call so I could be sure that no stones were left unturned. Upon dialoguing with the customer service representative, I was afforded subsidized internet services. When I got the first bill there was an unexpected balance of $0.00. Now wait a minute! What is going on? So, I called the company to verify the statement amount. I was informed that the company had a program that would be paying the balance after the subsidy each month. This resulted in a zero-dollar balance for the next six months. This benefit ended when I moved to another city and this plan could not be transferred to the new location. I never imagined that having a bill for $0.00 existed. This was way above my imagination and expectations. It is in these moments that the written Word of God becomes evident right before our eyes. Ephesians 3:20 states that God can do way above anything that we may ask or even imagine. This is exactly what God did for me; I thought getting a subsidized bill was great but then God did even greater. He exceeded my thoughts with a bill of $0.00 for six months. God will take care of His children. The only requirement is that we put Him first by loving Him with all our hearts, souls, and minds.

"And if God cares so wonderfully for wildflowers that are here today and thrown into the fire tomorrow, he will certainly care for you...

Seek the Kingdom of God above all else, and live righteously, and he will give you everything you need."

Matthew 6:30-33 (NLT)

Making the transition from Jamaica to the United States was a humbling experience. Coming to America was a vulnerable experience of leaving the island of my birth and walking into the unknown. All that was familiar diminished, and this new beginning meant finding my footing again. I assumed the role of a student, a student in life and in my craft. It felt like being left at sea without a glimpse of the shore in sight. Voracious waves crashed into my boat and my heart palpitated. Yet, I chose not to return to familiar shores but instead pursued uncharted waters. There were countless times when I was the apprentice learning to ride these waves on the go, but I was determined that I had come too far to turn back now. Learning the unspoken rules of a new environment is never easy. This meant doing research, asking many questions, making mistakes, making adequate preparations, coming in early, and burning the midnight oil.

Thankfully, I was able to pull from the toolkit my parents had furnished me with over the years through the lessons of determination. So, with tears, apprehension, ambition, curiosity, and my faith in God, I decided that I would endure to the end. I quickly realized the differences in the way of life and adapted to survive. I improved personally and professionally. Being exposed to diverse cultures shaped and enhanced my teaching methodologies, communication skills, and relational capacity. My perspicacity on life evolved as I immersed myself in this new experience. Life is not defined by limited idiosyncratic experiences but is an amalgamation of all our collective experiences.

During this phase, as soon as I got in my apartment, I literally dropped my bags, slid my feet from my shoes, and hit the ground on my knees. I petitioned God, letting Him know that I could not do this on my own and so I cried out to Him for help. I prayed consistent prayers asking for the wisdom, knowledge, and understanding to navigate this difficult chapter of my life. I can attest to the effectiveness of those fervent prayers.

> *"Confess your sins to each other and pray for each other so that you may be healed. The earnest prayer of a righteous person has great power and produces wonderful results."*
>
> James 5:16 (NLT)

Each day, I was dedicated to prayer as I cried out for God's help. Finally, I got a breakthrough where I started grasping, adapting, and honing the new skills needed to make progress. From that moment on, the struggle to acclimatize was aborted and I received strategy, creativity and innovation from the Lord. The consistent prayers brought me to a threshold, where I crossed over to a point of no return to the struggles. The scripture below tells us that the fear of the Lord is the beginning of all wisdom. The wisdom and creativity that galvanized my success through this period is attributed to my commitment to prayer.

> *"Fear of the Lord is the foundation of true wisdom. All who obey his commandments will grow in wisdom. Praise him forever!"*
>
> Psalm 111:10 (NLT)

Overall, taking on the journey to the United States made me realize the power of overcoming self-doubt and allowing myself to have this new experience and challenge. I would advise anyone to take the chance of allowing themselves to have enough new experiences and challenges. It takes courage to take on challenges, but the reward builds self-awareness, self- esteem, and personal development. The wisdom, self-improvement, and self-actualization on the other side of overcoming is priceless. My self-esteem has been elevated even more because I triumphed on this journey of stepping into the unknown by faith. This leap of faith led to a journey of self-discovery as I navigated rejection and solitude.

There were lots of ruminations on my childhood as I searched the archive of lessons from my parents. These archives served as toolkits that led to introspection and ultimately the reinvention of myself. This wisdom from my parents was reserved in a concealed toolkit I did not even recognize I had. Now in solitude, in a foreign land, with less than ideal experiences and inconveniences, it was time to unlock and utilize these gems. The solitude. The foreign land. The less than ideal experiences and inconveniences were all stimuli that coined me into the person I was becoming. These challenges influenced me to be excellent regardless of passive aggressive and indelicate environments. Behind the scenes, this experience covertly morphed my character and philosophies.

Choosing to live through the agony was not easy, but it was required to move toward my destiny. I was determined that I had come too far to give up on myself or to return home. Moreover, I could not give up on the path I believed God was taking me down. The rejection I endured could not be ignored. I have never felt such immense rejection in my life, but it built me. Psalm 119 expresses that times of suffering are good because they teach us to give attention to the principles of God. I did not crumble during this time of suffering, because I turned my focus on God.

"My suffering was good for me, for it taught me to pay attention to your decrees."

Psalm 119:71 (NLT)

When rejected, I was forced to embrace my identity and to really know who I am. This was building an indomitable confidence and self-worth. I was reading self-help books, listening to podcasts, participating in self-improvement challenges, and attending conferences to further develop my confidence. Deep down inside, I knew there was a purpose that must prevail and so I never gave up and continued to build myself. I was confident in who I am because of my confidence in God. I learned to be confident despite the hostility, because I turned my affections to my audience of One. Through this rejection I realized that favor should not be sought from man but only from God. Through it all, I learned to trust in Jesus, and I grew to know him more.

It was during these five years I truly learned to rely on God. My faith was increased experientially and through reading the Word of God. Intentional time was spent in scriptures and being involved in a Christian community. Eventually I started sharing exhortations in said Christian community from which the *Teach the Nations; Build the Church* podcast was birthed.

According to Charles Dickens, *"It was the best of times, it was the worst of times."* Coming to America was the best time of my life and the worst time of my life. It was the worst of times because I have never experienced such cold-shouldering and isolation. Inversely, it was the best of times because it was throughout this wilderness experience that purpose was perceived, pursued, and produced the 2.0 version of myself.

During these five years of isolation I went to therapy, wrote this book, found purpose while in solitude, worked on my emotional wellness, experienced healing, met God the provider, learned to stand in courage with boldness, grew deeper in Christ, embarked on a journey of self-love and discovery, interceded for family members, grew in patience, endurance, and love, learned to be slow to anger, and appreciated delayed gratification. Without faith it is impossible to please God (Hebrews 11:6). But the thing about faith is that God does not show us the fine print that says "conditions apply." I took a leap of faith in coming to America, but never considered the magnitude of the conditions that applied.

I sojourned to teach in North Carolina for five years, but so much more occurred during this time. Being isolated, uncomfortable, and inconvenienced for five years required submission to God's greater plan. Taking this leap out of my comfort zone was a tempestuous experience, but was necessary to unearth purpose and to become a greater version of myself. Even though it was a daunting decision to take this step, I took the step anyway. This was an ideal representation of courage in action. Some of the most fulfilling experiences ensue from the times we step out of our comfort zone. I had desired a change for so long, but was trapped in everyday routines. Stepping out in courage and boldness provoked the hidden and dormant aspects of myself that birthed purpose.

By faith I took the risk; by faith I survived the risk!

"Have I not commanded you? Be strong and courageous. Do not be afraid; do not be discouraged, for the Lord your God will be with you wherever you go."

Joshua 1:9 (NIV)

Broken Bricks Still Build

Chapter 10

—∞—

Crushed Again

By and by, when the morning comes,
when the saints of God are gathered home,
we'll tell the story, how we've overcome,
for we'll understand it better by and by.

- Charles Albert Tindley

Believing a promise when the prospects are dim feels like standing in the dark and being told that light exists. So, what do we do while we stand in the dark? We trust and wait. The only way to endure the wait is to trust that God's goodness will manifest regardless of the odds. In the dark we grapple with fragments of uncertainties and questions but no answers. This is the moment we are required to trust God even when nothing makes sense. It is the time to believe that all things are working together for good for those who love God (Romans 8:28). When I was standing in a dark part of my journey with a heavy heart, I humbled myself to the truth that His ways are not my ways (Isaiah 55:8). I was reassured that God's ways are higher than mine when I remembered Him as the Ancient of Days, the One who existed before the existence of days and creation. So, who am I not to trust that His ways and thoughts are higher than mine? I started to esteem His thoughts as superior to my limited thoughts. I recognized that my thoughts cannot be compared to His thoughts. This truth reveals how skewed our thoughts are when compared to His. As far as the heavens are from the Earth, so are His ways and thoughts above mine. How far is that? It cannot be measured. We cannot figure out God's mind, thoughts, or ways. Our only reassurance is to believe that His ways are always better and far exceed whatever we think (Ephesians 3:20).

"For my thoughts are not your thoughts, neither are your ways my ways, saith the Lord.

For as the heavens are higher than the earth, so are my ways higher than your ways, and my thoughts than your thoughts."

Isaiah 55:8-9 (KJV)

"Now unto him that is able to do exceeding abundantly above all that we ask or think, according to the power that worketh in us..."

Ephesians 3:20 (KJV)

In between the promise and the manifestation was a lonely journey where the silence was so loud. It is the part of the journey where I waited and continued believing without evidence of the promise. I did not understand how the pieces of the mosaic would assemble in the end, but I waited in confidence on the Lord.

"Wait on the Lord: be of good courage, and he shall strengthen thine heart: wait, I say, on the Lord."

Psalm 27:14 (KJV)

Can you imagine telling the pitch-black sky that the sun exists? Do you think this darkness would believe that the sun truly exists? How can a sky so dark become so bright? As I continued believing God for a particular promise, I pondered these thoughts. Believing a promise in the dark is just the beginning of the journey to see the promise. While on this journey, we must continue to believe that the promise will come to pass. Many people do not see the promise because they become discouraged about the odds and abort their journey. Seeing the promise means walking in moments of not yet and uncertainty while waiting on God to complete the process He started.

Honestly, I became tired while waiting. I was physically, mentally and spiritually exhausted. There were even times when I wondered if I would ever see the fulfillment of the promise. In this chapter I will share how I navigated waiting on God for the promise of healing. At the beginning of this healing journey, I could not fathom how this predicament would reveal the goodness of God. However, I stayed on course and continued believing that His ways and thoughts are higher than mine.

In December 2021, I went to the doctor for my annual physical exam. I was not prepared to hear one of the most devastating pieces of news in my life. After the doctor's visit and follow-up labs, I received three diagnoses. One of the most painful impacts of the diagnoses received is that my reproductive health was in jeopardy. This was challenging to handle because one of my greatest desires is to become a wife and the mother of many children. Many women around me were getting married and were having babies. Unfortunately, for me the results showed that my reproductive system was compromised with a large mass. A tumor. A fibroid. My test results were exacerbated when I received further feedback from my doctor about other tests done. In the second diagnosis, I was informed that abnormalities were observed that were linked to cancer. The third diagnosis was also critical, but treatment options were much simpler.

I was drowning in dejection and was now in a broken state again. What do you do when you leave your doctor with three diagnoses and pamphlets in your hand? The medical implications of the different diagnoses were obvious, but I was not ready for the psychosocial impacts. I was plagued with debilitating thoughts that poked at my mental health and even my social life. I avoided certain conversations and isolated myself from any situation that would irritate this wound. The signs and symptoms of the diagnosis made me very conscious about my body. I did not wear certain clothes and even dealt with body shame. I was uncomfortable in my own body as I could see and feel the evidence of sickness. In my mind I thought I was unfit for marriage, because who wants a woman whose womb is compromised? I was unprepared for the psychological struggles that were associated with the diagnoses.

Eventually, I broke the news to my family, and I could hear and feel the disappointment from them. But I did not tell them the whole diagnosis. I wanted to hide it. My mother, who has always been a praying woman, dedicated time to praying and fasting for my healing and my father affirmed me. I clearly remember the encouraging words of my father. "I am not my own, I belong to Jesus." He added, "Be still and know that I am God." I was particularly reassured by this because previously I had asked God, "What are You really saying about the matter?" In that moment all that came to my mind was to be still. So, hearing this from my father felt like confirmation to be still and know that He is God. With this support from both parents, I felt a bit more empowered to tackle this part of the journey.

The facts kept ringing in my ears that there was a large tumor growing in my womb. I was crushed and my heart felt like it had been ripped from chest. My reproductive prospects felt threatened as doctors mentioned surgery, biopsy, high risk pregnancies, and uncertainties about becoming pregnant. Having to consider the side effects of various procedures was not easy. It was just too much to think about in a short time. In this phase, I was so broken and felt like everything was shattered to pieces. Many nights I wept miserably. I felt like I was about to go into another cycle of depression. Navigating this season in the pandemic without direct support of family and friends was challenging. I said to myself, this is the worst year of my life. I knew my mental state was in danger and I could not withstand this in my own strength.

As I thought about all that was happening, I heard the lyrics to "New Wine" by Hillsong. The lyrics reassured me that even though I felt so crushed, God was extracting something new out of me. I was encouraged that this season of crushing was producing a new thing in me, and so I had hope again. I believed again that there was something greater that would come from all of this. I turned my eyes to the hills where my help and strength come from. I gave my attention to God, who is our present help in times of trouble.

"I will lift up mine eyes unto the hills, from whence cometh my help.

My help cometh from the Lord, which made heaven and earth."

Psalm 121:1-2 (KJV)

God is our refuge and strength, a very present help in trouble."

Psalm 46:1 (KJV)

On December 23, 2021, I decided to fast from 6:00 a.m. to 6 p.m. I did this fast every day for the remainder of the year. I diligently fasted and prayed, seeking God for strength because I felt like I would lose my mind. I kept feeding my mind with scriptures and spent hours seeking God. There were times in prayer that I felt like I was protesting in the spirit to seek justice. I had to keep my mind in the Word of God because it felt impossible to process all this bad news in my head. I read Philippians 4:8 fervently to help refocus my thoughts.

"Finally, brethren, whatsoever things are true, whatsoever things are honest, whatsoever things are just, whatsoever things are pure, whatsoever things are lovely, whatsoever things are of good report; if there be any virtue, and if there be any praise, think on these things."

Philippians 4:8 (KJV)

In conjunction with this verse, the story of the children of Israel played a major role in my forward thinking. This story helped me over this hurdle because even though the Red Sea was right before their eyes, mountains were on both sides, and Pharoah and his chariots were behind them, the Israelites kept moving forward. This gave me the fuel to keep thinking positively despite being surrounded with doubt, fear, and bad news. It was only day two of the fast when God intentionally appealed to my faith to believe for a miracle through the voice of Bishop R.C. Blakes Jr. As I listened to a YouTube video he posted titled "He is the God of Miracles" my spirit broke and I was in disbelief at this coincidence. The primary stimulus for the fast was seeking the Lord for a miracle. My initial prompting to fast was now reinforced by the prophetic word released by R.C. Blakes. In his message Bishop Blakes said:

> God says to tell the people to elevate their expectations. There will be twelve days of miracles leading to December 31, 2021. For some of them this has been the worst days of their lives but in these last few days, God can move miraculously where this can be repackaged as the best year of your lives. Tell the people to expect the miraculous. Elevate your faith and expect God to do something uncommon and unusual in your life. Elevate your faith as an offering to God.

This well-timed video by R.C. Blakes was a set-up by God for me to contend for my faith. It felt as though this video gave me even more reason to pursue God in believing for a miracle. This video raised my expectancy to see a miracle from God in this current situation. In *Acres of Diamonds*, Pastor Jentezen Franklin writes:

> "If God is going to do something, He is going to look for people who have expectation. We need to start getting up on our tiptoes and expect God to do the impossible again. This is how we bind the spirit of negativism."[5]

5 Jentezen Franklin, *Acres of Diamonds* (2020). 135

Additionally, during these days of intense fasting and praying, God started to speak to me about completing my assignment of writing this book. I went to God about my health, but He started speaking about my purpose. God was reminding me that I still had a testimony to share. Grappling with this bad news, it was as though there was a huge disruption that had stopped everything in my life. I felt less of a woman, and I also felt like the unpopped popcorn in the bag. Just about everyone around me was getting married and starting to have children. But what did I have? A negative doctor's report and a tumor. I asked myself, what is the point in writing this book, anyway? I was rattled by all of this and contemplated stopping writing this book altogether. I was confused and could not fathom what was going on.

Then, for a moment I reflected on all that was already written. I recognized that the story so far was solid as a rock, and every part of it was held up on how God had been undergirding my story the whole time. So, when I realized that what was already written was unshakable, I knew I had to continue writing. Every part of it could stand, regardless of the turn my story had taken with this bad news. I even questioned my faith in God and asked God "Why me?" Nevertheless, when I looked back at my life and saw the evidence of God, I knew I had to continue believing even though the odds were against me. I came into an even stronger agreement with God that even if I do not have children or get married, I will still carry out what He requires me to do. So, even though I felt like I was at yet another crossroads in my life, I still managed to say, "Lord, let Your will be done even if this is my story." Holding on to your faith through pain is tough. However, because of our faith in God, we can be reassured that nothing is a surprise or unexpected to God, for all things are orchestrated and controlled by Him.

As the end of 2021 approached, I continued believing God for a miracle in fasting and prayer. It was the last Sunday of the year and I decided to go to church. A minister gave an exhortation about God the healer. When he introduced this topic, I looked at him with raised eyebrows and wide eyes. He shared from Mark 16:20, which emphasizes that signs should follow those who believe. During his message, he shared how on previous occasions he prayed for different individuals who later received their healing. As the sermon was concluded, the minister extended an invitation to anyone in need of healing to come to the altar. He emphasized that he would lay his hands on each person and pray for them. I remembered him saying that the healing may not be instantaneous but as we believe and go, we would receive our healing. So, I went to the altar along with other members of the congregation and the minister prayed for and laid his hands on each of us. I refused to believe that this was a coincidence. Everything seemed to be coming together, the prayer and fasting for a miracle, Bishop RC Blakes releasing a prophetic word about the God of miracles, and now this minister specifically exhorts the congregation to believe in God the healer. This sequence of events could not be relegated as mere coincidence, it was providence in plain sight. Even Albert Einstein once said, *"Coincidence is God's way of staying anonymous."* As I continued in prayer and fasting for the remainder of the year, I heavily meditated on Psalm 27:13-14 that gave me the reassurance that believing to see the goodness of God in my life is what will sustain me during this time. The shield of faith from Ephesians 6 was my defense as I continued believing God for a miracle.

> *"I would have lost heart, unless I had believed that I would see the goodness of the Lord In the land of the living.*
>
> *Wait on the Lord; be of good courage, and He shall strengthen your heart; wait, I say, on the Lord!"*
>
> Psalm 27:13-14 (NKJV)

The year 2022 has marked my life forever. Numerous trips and consultations were made to the doctor and specialists based on my diagnoses. I nervously went through several scans and additional tests still expecting a miracle. I hoped for the best treatment option that would preserve my uterus. On one hand, I believed I was on the cusp of a miracle, but on the other, there were three diagnoses. How do you handle expectancy and despair in the same heart? We choose faith and believe to see God's goodness. Waiting for the promise takes time, but I could not remain downcast or lose hope in the wait. Instead, I had to develop confidence that God will indeed make me a witness to the goodness He has promised in my life.

Psalm 27 taught me through this experience that waiting on God requires patience. It was the part of the journey where it looked like nothing was happening. The odds seemed to be against me; it was simply a moment where it felt like there was no light at the end of the tunnel and all hope was lost. Amid all the darkness, I used my faith to push past the darkness. I continued believing that God would make me a witness to the promise of His goodness and that the ultimate reward was delayed gratification. The wait taught me to hear God in the dark. It felt like I was being tested in fog, where challenges were aimed at me that I could not understand. My only way out was to pull on the armor of fasting, prayer, and putting scriptures to the test for myself. I kept believing to see God's goodness even when it was not my turn to testify. Waiting for the promise is the part of the journey where we triumph in the dark. Sometimes it felt like waiting in vain, but waiting builds patience and patience is faith. It takes courage to wait, because there is a confident expectation of what is to come. And if we are courageous enough to wait, we are stronger and more resilient than we think.

Waiting on God brought me to the consciousness that I was not in control. This season really solidified that His thoughts are not mine and neither are His ways. God's ways supersede anything I can plan for my life. In the flesh I was disappointed, but in the spirit, I was trusting His plans, ways, and thoughts. To avoid being overwhelmed, I chose to look the other way. Looking the other way meant keeping my mind on things that encouraged my faith, like Philippians 4:8 and writing this book. I refused to focus on negativity. Focusing on negativity would only influence a pessimistic mindset.

As I became more intentional about looking the other way, I learnt to be a good steward over my days. I was more purposeful in managing my time and continued working on the assignment right in front of me. During this chapter, my faith was challenged and stretched. I found myself out on a limb, believing God for a miracle. It was this experience that afforded me the opportunity to witness the wonderful works of the Lord in the deep.

> *"Those who go down to the sea in ships, who do business on great waters,*
>
> *They see the works of the Lord, And His wonders in the deep."*
>
> Psalm 107:23-24 (NKJV)

This chapter confirms that Jehovah Rapha, the Lord my Healer, exists. As the minister gave an exhortation about God the healer, I was empowered to continue believing for a miracle. I believed and kept living, despite the facts. After being referred to a specialist for advanced care, I was given a six-month interval for repeat testing. From this specialist I was referred again to another specialist to undergo a procedure. However, it was seven months before I got results from the first specialist. Finally, I received correspondence from my doctor, and the results were normal; there were no abnormalities. The specialist ordered a follow-up test in another six months. When the results became available in 2023, I anxiously logged into the patient portal and the results were normal. Then in 2024 the tests were done again, and the results were normal.

As for the procedure, I had a very rough recovery. After the anesthesia wore off and even with other pain medications it was the most excruciating pain I had ever sustained. I am still walking out this part of the healing journey. The imaging from the post-procedural scans have shown positive results and the signs and symptoms in my body have drastically improved. How do you respond when God fulfills His promises?

To God be the glory, great things he has done!

So loved he the world that he gave us his Son,

who yielded his life an atonement for sin,

and opened the life-gate that all may go in.

Praise the Lord, praise the Lord, let the earth hear His voice!

Praise the Lord, praise the Lord, let the people rejoice!

Oh, come to the Father, through Jesus the Son,

And give Him the glory, great things He hath done.

-Fanny Crosby

I would have fainted had I not believed to see the goodness of the Lord in the land of the living. I can confidently testify that I have seen the goodness of the Lord because I believed. Going through this tough experience was a prerequisite for elevating my faith in God. It was a time of perseverance until I saw the goodness of God. We are required to go through difficult seasons to know God for ourselves. Having gone through the storm and surviving to the end, I can boldly say I know that God still heals. In Job 42:5 (NLT) Job said, "I had only heard about you before, but now I have seen you with my own eyes." From my experience I have heard of God the Healer, but now I have seen with my own eyes that He is the Healer.

> *"I wait for the Lord, my whole being waits, and in His word, I put my hope. I wait for the Lord more than watchmen wait for the morning, more than watchmen wait for the morning."*

Psalm 130:5-6

Chapter 11

---∞---

The Dichotomy of Singleness

All to Jesus I surrender,
All to Him I freely give;
I will ever love and trust Him,
In His presence daily live.

Judson W. Van DeVenter

The single season of my life allowed me to appreciate the advantages of being single, while recognizing the benefits a partner could potentially offer. In my earlier years of being single after my relationship with Keith, I still wanted to be loved. In retrospect I was still broken and was searching to fill a void. Let us look at how the story of Gomer resonated with that part of my journey. In Hosea chapter 3, Gomer squandered her sexuality even though she was married. Instructed by God, her husband Hosea bought her back as his wife despite her choices. This resonated with my journey because similarly, I made the poor relational choice of entering a non-marital relationship with Keith. I believe Gomer was trying to fill a void. Comparably, I too wanted to fill a void because even after I fled that relationship, I still desired a partner. What was Gomer looking for? What was I still looking for? Was it love or support? I am not sure. For so long I still desired to have a partner in my life and to have a family. Time elapsed and the desire never came to fruition, and I saw where hope deferred made my heart sick. So, gradually I started to loosen the grip on said desires. During this yearning desire I collided with Jesus. It was the inflection point where my desires were redirected to Christ, and I have never looked back since. Jesus bought me back when He saved and transformed my heart. For so long I sought for affection in the wrong places just like Gomer, until Jesus showed up and said "Enough."

By contrast, as I continued in singleness my perspective on love morphed. I had been healed to the extent where my desire was not solely to be loved but to give love. This change in desire was because of the transformation and renewal of my mind. I became confident that I am loved by God, and I received said love. I experienced the of love God and I am still living in it today. Even though I was embracing singleness, there was still the desire for support from a spouse. I constantly asked God, "Why is this desire so persistent? Why can't I be totally contented with Your love?" I asked these questions for months. Finally, I heard it's not that love for a partner is unimportant; all God requires is that I love Him first. Matthew 22 tells us that the first and greatest commandment is to love the Lord our God with all our hearts.

"Jesus said unto him, thou shalt love the Lord thy God with all thy heart, and with all thy soul, and with all thy mind. This is the first and great commandment.

Matthew 22:37-38 (KJV)

Based on my journey I have realized that love cannot be reciprocated unless it is experienced. Experiencing God's love was a personal encounter that equipped me to love myself and then others. How can we receive and reciprocate true love if we do not know the love of Christ? A personal walk with Christ where His love is experienced teaches love, patience, faithfulness, forgiveness, grace, and kindness. Having this firsthand experience of true love, all I wanted to do was exercise the muscle of expressing love. There was a necessity to give back the love that nursed me back to health. My cup was full, and I wanted to pour it into someone else's life, which I believed would be through having a family. This would ultimately complete my journey of healing in pouring back the love I received from Christ. I felt ready to establish and build a family, but where was the partner? Many people were walking in their answered prayers of having a family, while I did not have answers to mine. This meant celebrating with others when it was not my turn. So, while I wait for the family, let me pour back into the lives of anyone reading this book. I hope that my story has been able to serve as a testimony and inspiration for whoever resonates with my journey.

As I continued wanting to establish a family, God started to show me the immense responsibilities associated with this desire. Having a family is more than taking cute family pictures and celebrating the birth of babies. In having a family, there are responsibilities of caring, providing, nurturing, and loving the children, etc. But there is also the direct responsibility of raising the children in the fear of the Lord. According to Deuteronomy 6, it is a requirement to teach our children the Word of the Lord. This was a responsibility I needed to make sure I was ready to be intentional about. This consciousness is needed to train up children who know and honor the Lord.

> *"These commandments that I give you today are to be on your hearts. Impress them on your children. Talk about them when you sit at home and when you walk along the road, when you lie down and when you get up."*
>
> Deuteronomy 6:6-7 (NIV)

Raising a family is no joke, because it requires the parents to be purposeful and thoughtful in the values they instill in their children. The lives of children should be impacted by Godly principles taught by their parents. Deuteronomy 6 further implies that parents and children should have a close relationship, where regular conversations should allow Godly principles to be transferred. Deuteronomy depicts this close relationship by encouraging parents to talk with their children about God's commandments at home, while walking on the road, when they lie down or get up. Through a close relationship, parents will have influence on the choices their children make and their faith in God. I became reflective on these other aspects of becoming a parent and got a chance to evaluate this desire.

In *Believe for It,* Cece Winans writes passionately about passing on faith to the next generation. Winans writes:

If we want to instill faith and godliness into our children and grandchildren, we must plant those seeds through our daily actions. We must read the Scripture and have conversations about it. We must talk about what God is doing in our lives. We must pray with our children and over them. We must model for them how we trust the Lord through trials. We must teach them to love their enemies. This is sowing to the Spirit, and it bears good fruit.[6]

Winans continues:

Passing on faith to the next generation requires work, but it's work worth doing, because the reward is great. And the best part is, we don't do the work alone.[7]

During my season of solitude, I thought more about submission. Since I desired marriage, it was logical to evaluate this concept of submission. In Ephesians 5, wives are expected to submit to their husbands as they submit to the Lord. As I reflected on this text, I realized that in a marriage I would be required to view and accept a husband as the head. The scripture further highlights the necessity to respect the husband since he governs the union. Having studied this chapter, I have seen a greater reason to be selective in choosing a spouse. Taking that into consideration, it would be imperative to choose a spouse that I will submit to because of my respect and honor for him. I have attuned myself to the attributes needed to complement a husband in marriage. By default, committing to a marriage means I would need to align myself to said attributes of a wife.

---

6. Cece Winans, *Believe for It* (2022).74
7. Cece Winans, *Believe for It* (2022).87

"For wives, this means submit to your husbands as to the Lord. For a husband is the head of his wife as Christ is the head of the church. So again I say, each man must love his wife as he loves himself, and the wife must respect her husband."

Ephesians 5:22-23;33 (NLT)

Singleness provided the opportunity for me to view a spouse through the original lens of the Creator without the biases of society. I can write from this perspective because I had the opportunity to navigate life alone. In embracing the single season, I became more resolute to wait for a partner who honors God. Throughout my singleness I realized that choosing a spouse is a very selective process that should not be taken for granted. It would be unwise to deviate from this mindset. Previously, I made the incautious relational choice of being with Keith. Therefore, I will make wiser choices for my future spouse. As my season of solitude continued, I learned to acknowledge and appreciate the value a man is intended to bring to the life of a woman. In Ephesians 5, the intended value of the man is outlined. The husband is expected to love his wife just as Christ loves the church. The husband should love and not cause harm to his wife. The text further alludes that the husband should prioritize his wife by leaving his parents and being united with his wife. Moreover, it provides an exemplary framework and standards to consider when selecting a husband. From Ephesians 5, it can be inferred that Christ operates in the role of a shepherd for the church. According to the forementioned scripture, Christ should be emulated by the husband. This suggests that the husband should assume the role of a shepherd who feeds and cares for his flock, through offering provision and protection for his wife, the weaker vessel.

"In this same way, husbands ought to love their wives as their own bodies. He who loves his wife loves himself. After all, no one ever hated their own body, but they feed and care for their body, just as Christ does the church— for we are members of his body. 'For this reason a man will leave his father and mother and be united to his wife, and the two will become one flesh.'"

Ephesians 5: 28-31 (NIV)

In 1 Peter 3:7, the woman is referred to as the weaker vessel. I have heard this phrase so many times but did not fully understand it. I gained a better understanding during my singleness. I realized that being the weaker vessel means that I am a delicate being who is to be cherished, loved intentionally, and protected. Being the weaker vessel does not equate to being inferior to the man. In fact, the forementioned scripture implores the husband to honor his wife because she is the weaker vessel and reminds him that she is a fellow heir of the grace of life.

"Likewise, ye husbands, dwell with them according to knowledge, giving honor unto the wife, as unto the weaker vessel, and as being heirs together of the grace of life; that your prayers be not hindered."

1 Peter 3: 7 (KJV)

The beauty about my singleness is that I had a lot of quiet time. Five years of my singleness were spent secluded in a rural community in North Carolina. There were no close-knit friends nor family, so I had time to just think and meditate. There was time to reflect on life, gain wisdom and insight from God. I believe God has given me insight on marriage. When a man and a woman are joined in marriage, it is like a duet. In this duet, the song is such a pleasure, with the blend of both voices singing melodious harmonies. Marriage is meant to be experienced as a blend of both individuals. The song can be sung by one partner, but it is made even more enjoyable by the harmony that each partner adds to the song.

The dominant narrative from singles was that the dating scene is dreadful and that all the good men are taken. I really did not have a point of reference, because I felt like I was in the hidden scenes. It seemed there was not even a modicum of testosterone in my path. However, I had the chance to reflect on this narrative and my question is "How do we know that all the men that are taken are good?" This inaccurate narrative has skewed the hope of many singles. I refuse to believe that all the good men are taken; certainly, there are many good men out there. I believe that at the right time my life will transition from singleness to having a family. Do I believe that love exists? Yes, I do. I take this stance on the premise of Song of Solomon 3:5 NLT *Promise me, O women of Jerusalem, by the gazelles and wild deer, not to awaken love until the time is right.* Since the text urges the daughters of Jerusalem not to awaken love until the time is right, it suggests that love exists, but the caveat is that love should not be awakened prematurely.

Being single for such a long time, there was an undeniable struggle with lust. This single season seemed like it was not about to change anytime soon. I had to learn to circumvent the persistent sexual urges that were like a hungry shark that kept circling back. I battled thoughts of yielding my members as instruments of unrighteousness. Fortunately, I was able to maintain celibacy as I navigated this period of singleness. Thank God I was in a season of isolation from everything and everyone that was familiar. God knows how to convict our hearts, and I have been convicted by Romans 6 on countless occasions during my singleness.

Do not let sin control the way you live; do not give in to sinful desires. Do not let any part of your body become an instrument of evil to serve sin. Instead, give yourselves completely to God, for you were dead, but now you have new life. So, use your whole body as an instrument to do what is right for the glory of God."

Romans 6:12-13 (NLT)

This single season was the perfect time for me to continue improving on my personal development. I took the time to immerse myself in books to widen my perspective and learn from the experience of others. Meeting inspirational individuals may never happen, but the opportunity to glean from their wisdom is possible by reading their books. My attendance to women empowering sessions for self-development, spiritual growth, and preparation for marriage were also good ways to invest in myself. During singleness, I had the chance to do things by myself like going to the movies, dinner, and even concerts. Singleness afforded me the opportunity to take on new adventures, like migrating to the United States. By immersing myself in a new culture I created memories and experienced a new way of life. Taking a solo vacation as a single woman was one of most memorable times of my life. It was the ideal occasion to reflect, unwind from the demands of life, and be refreshed. It gave me a chance to channel any thoughts out of my mind as I walked freely on the sandy beach and enjoyed a boat ride. The experience provided a necessary pause to the cares of life; I forgot about everything and everyone. As I looked back at those vacation photos, I am so glad I made those memories. I would do it all over again. Solo vacation—I recommend it!

As a single woman, I became more intentional about my finances by improving my financial literacy. I improved on my budgeting so I could have as much financial confidence as possible. I learned to be a good steward over my finances and continued to pay my tithes and offerings. I started the necessary research to inform my decisions that would benefit my financial future. In working on my financial independence, I became flexible in adjusting my shopping list, giving up paid entertainment pleasures or even cancelling trips. This mindset taught me to do without today for the delayed gratification of tomorrow. Moving in this direction was imperative for working towards financial goals like building an emergency fund and starting investments.

In conclusion, I dedicated this chapter to showcasing how I navigated my season of singleness. It was not the most comfortable season. However, once I started paying attention, I could perceive some of the benefits singleness had to offer. Solitude provides the opportunity to think clearly, evaluate life, and reflect on my decisions in life. I grew closer to God and gained Godly perspectives on relationships. Moreover, I discovered ways to traverse the lonely parts of singleness by filling the void with non-sexual pleasures like solo vacations, personal development through books, and working on my financial future. Additionally, going to therapy during singleness produced one of my greatest accomplishments in life: this book. Pursuing personal development in singleness really allowed me to witness the evolution of myself over time. Some tendencies were kept, others gradually faded away and new ones were acquired. I am undeniably pleased with the blooms of my singleness.

Chapter 12

---∞---

God of the Hills and Valleys

This is my story, this is my song,
Praising my Savior all the day long;
This is my story, this is my song,
Praising my Savior all the day long

Fanny Crosby

Throughout this journey called life, I have navigated numerous hills and valleys. In the valleys I experienced many moments of shame, disappointment, regret, and heartbreak. These were the moments that left me feeling broken, unworthy, and insufficient. The beauty of being broken is that the story is not over. We tend to believe the lie that this is it, but the story continues. These broken moments are steppingstones along the journey that help to configure and fortify us to endure this marathon called life. Our stories have the potential to evolve into unfathomable chapters because we never imagined that there could ever be a comeback from the seasons that break us. If we think about a valley, it is low land located between hills. This is great motivation that even though we experience low seasons, we know that hills and mountains do exist. A valley is not the destination. In taking a hike to the mountain top, walking through the valley is an absolute prerequisite. It may be an uphill climb, but the mountain does exist. As we go through the valley experience, we can be reassured that as tough and challenging as it is, God is with us.

> *"When you go through deep waters, I will be with you. When you go through rivers of difficulty, you will not drown. When you walk through the fire of oppression, you will not be burned up; the flames will not consume you."*

> Isaiah 43:2 (NLT)

Many times, I felt trapped in the broken moments because I could not imagine that an alternative even existed. I thought to myself that I could never bounce back from such a setback. I brainstormed ways of getting out, but every option and attempt seemed futile. In the broken moments, I grappled with hopelessness and despair because I felt isolated, forgotten, and alone. These moments felt everlasting, and I wondered if things would always be this way. The fact that I tried to have a breakthrough in my own strength was the reason it seemed impossible. The broken parts of my heart were mended during my faith journey as I walked with Christ.

Mary and Martha were broken and distraught by the death of their brother Lazarus. From a disheartened and limited perspective, these sisters thought that their current suffering was the end of the story. Initially, Mary and Martha could not see beyond this temporary death. They thought this valley experience was permanent. The sisters never anticipated that this moment of disappointment was orchestrated for them to see Jesus from an improved perspective. Jesus allowed these sisters to intentionally walk through sorrow to reveal that God's plans transcend the valley seasons. Jesus had a greater plan when the sisters thought it was over; He had the plan for Lazarus to live again. Similarly, when we walk through the valley seasons of brokenness, God has a greater plan for us to resurrect and live again. Jesus is showing us that it does not matter how bleak the valley may seem, His power will always override our current suffering. Even when all hope is gone and we think it is over, God can show up in our valley seasons to give life and hope again. Though the valley feels endless, there is a reward of gaining a new perspective of God. Jesus intentionally delayed for four days because He wanted to create the scenario of the impossible becoming possible through Him. God wants to intervene in the impossible moments when we have written off our situation as a lost case. He wants to intervene in the moments when we think it is too late. Though we are teary eyed, disappointed, and distressed like Mary and Martha, brighter days are ahead.

"When Jesus saw her weeping, and the Jews who had come along with her also weeping, he was deeply moved in spirit and troubled.

When he had said this, Jesus called in a loud voice,
'Lazarus, come out!' The dead man came out, his hands
and feet wrapped with strips of linen, and a cloth around
his face."

John 11:33:43 (NIV)

Is the valley such a bad place? Based on my experience, the valley seasons slowed me down where I was forced to reflect on the good and the bad times. Without these bumps in the road, I would have continued living without taking inventory of the events of my life. Many times, I underestimated the value of the highs and lows. We often miss the lessons that God is teaching us if we do not pause to have meaningful reflection. In general, we perceive the purpose of our experiences as we reflect, because insight is often achieved in hindsight. I can only imagine the insight that Mary and Martha received in hindsight after Lazarus was raised from the dead. The sisters did not receive the insight of this valley season until they were standing on the hill of Lazarus' resurrection. We do not know what we've really got until we are down in the valley and forced to reflect on how far we have come. The valley seasons tested my faith to determine if I truly believed. Do we only believe when there are sunny skies? Or do we still believe when the dark clouds of affliction set in?

In the valley, I felt wounded as a soldier on the battlefield. Nevertheless, I got back up and pressed through. I had to keep my mind on the things of God to keep a positive mindset. I was keeping my mind focused on the scriptures and being in the presence of God. The valley teaches us to endure tribulations and simultaneously builds our patience. It is tempting to mishandle the low seasons of life, but it is our responsibility to be good stewards over every life experience so that we reap the hidden rewards.

"And not only so, but we glory in tribulations also: knowing that tribulation worketh patience..."

Romans 5:3 (KJV)

There were many times in my brokenness that I wrestled with silent tears welling up in my heart. In those moments I wondered if God really heard my cry. I allowed sorrows to eclipse the reality that all along God saw and heard my cry. In 2 Kings 20, Hezekiah was extremely sick. He was visited by the prophet Isaiah who gave him a message from the Lord that he would not recover from his illness and would die. Upon hearing this message Hezekiah turned to the Lord in prayer and wept bitterly. I would like to emphasize the fact that Hezekiah wept bitterly. This suggests that he was broken and filled with sorrow. But once again, the story is not over. After Hezekiah prayed, the Lord sent another message through the prophet saying his prayer was heard, his tears were seen, and that he would be healed. Hezekiah's story is such an inspiration for when we find ourselves in brokenness and times of sorrow. The Lord hears our prayers, and He sees our tears. God does not only see our tears, but He bottles them and heals our hearts.

"You keep track of all my sorrows. You have collected all my tears in your bottle. You have recorded each one in your book."

Psalm 56:8 (NLT)

Hagar had a similar experience to Hezekiah, Mary, and Martha, which proves that God hears our cries in times of distress. Hagar was a servant to Abraham's wife Sarai. She was misused into having sexual relations with Abraham. When she became pregnant, she was mishandled in being treated harshly by Sarai. She eventually ran away and was in a state of distress. Hagar experienced God as the One who hears our cries and sees us in times of distress. It does not matter how low the valley is, God is able to reach and restore us. There is no place too low or dark for God to reach us. The Lord's hand is not short that He cannot save (Isaiah 59:1).

> *"Abram replied, 'Look, she is your servant, so deal with her as you see fit.' Then Sarai treated Hagar so harshly that she finally ran away.*
>
> *And the angel also said, 'You are now pregnant and will give birth to a son. You are to name him Ishmael (which means 'God hears'), for the Lord has heard your cry of distress.'*
>
> *Thereafter, Hagar used another name to refer to the Lord, who had spoken to her. She said, 'You are the God who sees me.' She also said, 'Have I truly seen the One who sees me?'"*
>
> Genesis 16: 6;11;13 (NLT)

Weeping may endure for a night, but joy comes in the morning (Psalm 30:5). This empowers us that though we walk through the valleys of life, there is a hill of triumph on the other side. There is still hope in the valley even when our faith is running low. God does not forsake us in the valley; He prunes, shapes, and rebuilds us.

God was patient with me in the valley of sin, but today I stand on the hills of redemption. I suffered in the valley of domestic abuse and depression, but today I stand on the hills of freedom and restoration. Battling the valley of sickness was difficult, but I met Jehovah Rapha on the hills of healing. I struggled in the valley of bitterness and unforgiveness, but I learned to extend grace when I looked to the hills of Calvary. In the valley of waiting, I asked with uncertainty "why me" but then I stumbled onto the hills of purpose and destiny. Though I walked in the valley of rejection, I perceived the hills of my identity. The past valley of my brokenness gave birth to hills of confidence. The valley of wrong decisions built the hills of wisdom. From the valley of shame and timidness, I made it to the hills of being a published author with the courage to tell my story.

Since writing this book, I have recognized that I wanted to hide two of the most crucial events in my life. I wanted to hide the story of my abusive relationship and the diagnosis received from my doctor. I wanted to hide them because of shame, fear, and embarrassment. I have now seen that my attempt to hide my stories was contorting purpose and obscuring the miracle of healing in my life. This perspective was preventing me from honoring God in the valley seasons of my life. The desire to hide eroded my reverence, because I became so blind to the blessing. I took surviving the valley season lightly, because the whole time I had a chip on my shoulder asking "why me." Now being on the other side of testifying to the goodness of God, I have brought glory to the God of the hills and valleys. I am grateful that I submitted myself to this assignment of sharing my story, for God knows the plans He has for me (Jeremiah 29:11). My testimony has been preserved to spread the gospel of the goodness of God.

God is faithful, for He takes us through the hills and valleys. I thought I would have fainted, but He sustained and empowered me through the valley seasons of a broken home, career disappointment, a harrowing romance, sexual exploitation, domestic abuse, broken self-esteem, rejection, isolation, and sickness. Even though we are challenged with doubt and uncertainties in the valley, we must believe that we will see the goodness of the Lord in the Land of the living. Being sustained in the hills and valleys was possible because my hope is built on nothing less than Jesus' blood and righteous.

My hope is built on nothing less
Than Jesus' blood and righteousness
I dare not trust the sweetest frame
But wholly lean on Jesus' name

On Christ the solid rock I stand
All other ground is sinking sand
All other ground is sinking sand

-Edward Mote

Epilogue

As we navigate life, we encounter circumstances that shatter our hopes and dreams. Feeling disappointed and hopeless, we tend to believe it's the end of our stories. Though we are broken, our stories continue and will evolve as we rebuild our lives from the fragments of our past. Despite experiences that erode our confidence and impair our mental health and outlook on life, all is not lost. We can be reassured that these seasons are only temporary, and brighter days are ahead. Pain and brokenness won't last, for joy comes in the morning. With a surrendered heart to Christ He heals, restores, and stitches up the wounds of our broken hearts through the redemption He provides. The light of Christ liberates us from the past chains of depression, pain, and despair.

About the Author

Shawna-Kay Scarlett is the founder of the *Teach the Nations; Build the Church* podcast. As a Christian podcaster, she undertakes the mandate of sharing the gospel of Jesus Christ to all nations. The aim of her podcast is to unpack hidden principles from scriptures and make disciples of all nations. Shawna-Kay was born in Trelawny, Jamaica, where she spent most of her life with her parents and four siblings.

Shawna-Kay is an international science educator who has contributed to the welfare of the whole human race by impacting the lives of students internationally. With a decade in education, she utilizes her expertise in pedagogy to prepare her students to be college and career ready. Her high esteem for education is inspired by the motto of her alma mater, *Ignorance Enslaves, Knowledge Liberates*. Shawna-Kay is a graduate of the Mico University College in Kingston, Jamaica, where she achieved her pedagogical credentials. She is light-hearted, enjoys listening to music and playing the piano. She loves to cook, bake, and her favorite Jamaican cuisines include beef patties, curried goat with rice and peas, and sweet potato pudding.

Broken Bricks Still Build is her debut publication.

Instagram: Shawna-Kay Scarlett

 Facebook: Shawna- Kay Scarlett

 YouTube: Teach the Nations; Build the Church

 Spotify: Teach the Nations; Build the Church